DISCIPLE/ DISCIPLE-MAKER

And Other Writings

JOSEPH W. SEGREE

WESTBOW
PRESS®
A DIVISION OF THOMAS NELSON
& ZONDERVAN

WestBow Press books may be ordered through booksellers or by contacting:

WestBow Press
A Division of Thomas Nelson & Zondervan
1663 Liberty Drive
Bloomington, IN 47403
www.westbowpress.com
844-714-3454

Scripture quotations in books 1, 2 (except chapter 5), and 4 of this collection are from the New American Standard Bible (NASB), © The Lockman Foundation, 1960, 1962, 1963, 1966, 1971, 1972, 1975, 1977.

Scripture quotations in books 3, 5, and chapter 5 of book 2 are from the Holy Bible: New International Version (NIV) ©1973, 1978, 1984 by International Bible Society, used by permission of Zondervan Publishing House, all rights reserved.

A few quotations are from the King James Version (KJV) and the New King James Version (NKJV).

ISBN: 978-1-6642-9218-5 (sc)
ISBN: 978-1-6642-9217-8 (e)

Print information available on the last page.

WestBow Press rev. date: 02/28/2023

"My Father is glorified by this, that you bear much fruit,
and so prove to be My disciples."
—John 15:8

To Alma, my wife of fifty-four years, for encouraging me to write and for her many helpful suggestions in the editing of this book.

CONTENTS

PREFACE

The Bible says, "If anyone gives even a cup of cold water to one of these little ones because he is my disciple, I tell you the truth, he will certainly not lose his reward" (Matt. 10:42). We can do nothing greater to ensure that heavenly treasure will be credited to our account than to bring together these two things that will endure forever: the Word of God and the souls of people. Not until we reach heaven will we realize the degree to which we have impacted others for Christ. May we be able to say to some on that day, "For who is our hope or joy or crown of exultation? Is it not even you, in the presence of our Lord Jesus at His coming? For you are our glory and joy" (1Thess. 2:19–20).

The titles in this collection represent five biblical applications for the Christian's life, each of which relates directly or indirectly to the theme of laying up treasure in heaven by investing in the spiritual well-being of others.

Disciple/Disciple-Maker: Reading the New Testament, one can hardly miss the urgency and the clarity of Jesus' call. He doesn't call people to join an organization, to follow an ethic, a new teaching, or even a way of life but to come and follow Him. Jesus commissioned His followers to go make disciples of all the nations. This book is about becoming a true disciple of Jesus Christ and helping others become His disciples as well.

The Biblical Meaning of Greatness: Jesus defines greatness as humility and servanthood. He Himself is the supreme example of both! The message of the humble servant being the greatest in the kingdom of God is much needed in this day of Christian stars and celebrities.

Life in the Marketplace: This book addresses this often-asked question "Is it possible to integrate my work and my ministry in such a way as to find fulfillment in both?" Here the reader will find a sound biblical view of this issue, along with practical suggestions for effectively representing the Lord Jesus Christ in the workplace.

The Problem of Tares: The parable of the Wheat and the Tares is the backdrop for five serious mistakes committed by churches today as part of Satan's strategy for sowing tares among the wheat—counterfeit Christians among the genuine. As one notable Christian leader described it, "This message is a strong exhortation which needs to be heard in this age of relativism."

The Doctrine of Rewards: This scripture-filled study is based upon the principle that grace does not eliminate accountability. There are eternal consequences for temporal behavior. Every child of God must therefore examine the conduct of his or her life in light of this profound biblical truth.

The books in this collection were written for Christians. It is important to emphasize this from the outset. The life of discipleship outlined in these writings is a supernatural life. We do not have the power in ourselves to live it. The pathway to true discipleship begins when a person is born again. Only when we are born again do we receive the strength to live as Jesus taught. It begins when the following events occur:

1. When a person realizes that he* is sinful, lost, and helpless before God.
2. When he acknowledges that he cannot save himself by good character or good works.
3. When he believes that the Lord Jesus Christ died as his substitute on the cross.
4. When, by a definite decision of faith, he acknowledges Jesus Christ as his only Lord and Savior.

Before reading any further, ask yourself these questions: "Have I been born again? Have I become a child of God by faith in Jesus Christ?" If you have not, ask Him now to come into your life as your Lord and Savior. Then determine to obey Him in all that He has commanded, whatever the cost may be.

I sincerely hope that you will find *Disciple/Disciple-Maker* meaningful, stimulating, and applicable to your own life. Toward this end, I am pleased to dedicate it to the praise and glory of our great God and Savior, Jesus Christ.

*Author's note: While all the material in this book is applicable to men and women alike, the masculine gender is used for all singular pronouns (he, him, and his).

BOOK 1

Disciple/Disciple-Maker

CONTENTS

"Go into all the world and preach the gospel to all creation."
—Mark 16:15

INTRODUCTION

Disciple/Disciple-Maker is about becoming a disciple of Jesus Christ and helping others become disciples. Jesus calls people today, as He called them more than two thousand years ago, not to join an organization, to follow an ethic, a new teaching, or even a way of life. He calls us to Himself. In the Gospels, Jesus lays out simply and in no uncertain terms specific requirements for being His disciple. He also commissioned them, as He does us, to make disciples. When these men were ready, He sent them out to evangelize the world!

Should disciple-making be a priority or even a part of every Christian's life? What is our motivation or incentive to do so? Jesus issued three commandments that speak directly to these questions. We know them as (1) the Great Commandment (Mark 12:28–31); (2) the Great Commission (Matt. 28:19–20); and (3) the Great Commitment (Matt. 16:24). Taken together, these represent a powerful mandate for every Christian to be involved in the ministry of making disciples.

Disciple-making is a personal ministry to be carried out by people, not programs. It is to be carried out by someone and not by something. Disciples cannot be mass produced. We cannot drop people into a program and see disciples emerge at the end of the production line. It takes time to make disciples. It takes individual, personal attention. It takes hours of prayer for them. It takes patience and understanding.

Disciple-making is also a fruitful ministry. All living beings reproduce after their own kind: animals, plants—everything. In the same way, God's plan for evangelizing the world is through spiritual reproduction and multiplication. Every born-again Christian has the wonderful privilege and duty of bringing spiritual life to others. Spiritual life is transmitted through us, people who are spiritually alive! The eternal, incorruptible seed of everlasting life is in you and me.

"Whatever works best," disciple-making methods based upon practical rather than theoretical considerations, should be our mindset. In other words, our approach and plan must be tailored to the individual. The final section of *Disciple/Disciple-Maker* contains twenty-four practical, proven suggestions relevant to this ministry. It also lists many suggestions and helpful hints pertaining to the devotional life—our daily quiet time of prayer, Bible reading, and meditation upon the scriptures.

SECTION 1

Discipleship Sought

CHAPTER 1

THE CALL TO DISCIPLESHIP

"And He said to them, 'Follow Me, and I will make you fishers of men.'"

—Matthew 4:19

Reading the New Testament, one cannot miss the urgency and the clarity of Jesus' call. He spoke directly and succinctly to His listeners with an invitation to come to Him. His message never wavered. "I am the Way; follow Me."

But His invitation comes with a condition. It must be on His terms. These are set forth in the Gospels with simplicity and sometimes severity. This chapter and the one that follows are about the call and cost of following Jesus.

Consider the following features of Jesus' call to discipleship:

Jesus called men individually.

Jesus attracted the crowds with His teaching, preaching, and supernatural acts. They were amazed at the words He spoke and the miracles He performed. Many of the people accompanied Jesus largely for what they could get: healing, health, bread, fish, and other things. But Jesus called men for what He would enable them to become and what He wanted them to do. Salvation for the world began with twelve men whom He individually trained and sent out to preach the Gospel. Just as an infectious disease is transmitted from one person to another, so is the message of salvation spread—one person telling another and another.

Without hesitation, Jesus' first disciples left their nets—their jobs, families, and other worldly attachments—to become His disciples. This would eventually lead to their persecution and martyrdom.

Matthew recorded the calling of the first disciples.

> Now as Jesus was walking by the Sea of Galilee, He saw two brothers, Simon who was called Peter and Andrew his brother, casting a net into the sea; for they were fishermen. And He said to them, "Follow Me and I will make you fishers of men." Immediately they left their nets and followed Him. Going on from there He saw two other brothers, James the son of Zebedee, and John his brother, in the boat with Zebedee their father, mending their nets; and He called them. Immediately they left the boat and their father, and followed Him. (Matt. 4:18–22)

Jesus invested most of His time, energy, and attention in these four men plus eight others. They were the sole objects of His personal disciple-making ministry. He spent three years with them, yet one eventually betrayed Him. An important lesson can be learned from Jesus' example. If the Lord Himself concentrated upon just these few, can we expect to do more? Our goals and expectations must be realistic. Yet if we should continue this kind of ministry long term, imagine what an impact we might have for Christ and His kingdom!

Jesus said, "You did not choose Me but I chose you, and appointed you that you would go and bear fruit, and that your fruit would remain, so that whatever you ask of the Father in My name He may give to you" (John 15:16). Disciples cannot be mass produced. A preacher or Sunday school teacher may contribute to the disciple-making ministry in a church, but he cannot make disciples solely from the pulpit or in the classroom. Disciple-making, at best, always involves one person investing in another. This was how Jesus did it.

In calling disciples, Jesus made no distinction
between salvation and discipleship.

This may be the most misunderstood principle of discipleship in the church today. How else can one explain the sad fact that relatively few in the masses of "saved" people can rightfully be labeled "true disciples"? Jesus called men to action—to do something, to become devoted followers, and to obey His commands.

Luke recorded the following story:

> A wealthy young ruler questioned Him, saying, "Good Teacher, what shall I do to inherit eternal life?"
>
> And Jesus said to him, "Why do you call Me good? No one is good except God alone. You know the commandments, 'Do not commit adultery, do not murder, do not steal, do not bear false witness, honor your father and mother.'"
>
> And he said, "All these things I have kept from my youth."
>
> When Jesus heard this, He said to him, "One thing you still lack; sell all that you possess and distribute it to the poor, and you shall have treasure in heaven; and come, follow Me." But when he had heard these things, he became very sad, for he was extremely rich.
>
> And Jesus looked at him and said, "How hard it is for those who are wealthy to enter the kingdom of God! For it is easier for a camel to go through the eye of a needle than for a rich man to enter the kingdom of God."
>
> They who heard it said, "Then who can be saved?"
>
> But He said, "The things that are impossible with people are possible with God." (Luke 18:18–27)

Jesus did not tell the young man how to be saved but rather what salvation really meant. It was a one-time call to both salvation and discipleship. Andrew Murray addressed it in terms of total submission to Christ.

Giving up one's whole life to Him, for Him alone to rule and order it; taking up His yoke, and submitting to be led and taught, to learn of Him; abiding in Him, to be and do only what He wills—these are the conditions of discipleship without which there can be no thought of maintaining the rest that was bestowed on first coming to Christ. The rest is in Christ, and not something He gives apart from Himself, and so it is only in having Him that the rest can really be kept and enjoyed.[1]

Jesus' call demanded a thoughtful, if not immediate, response.

As noted previously, Matthew said these first disciples left their nets immediately. Levi likewise left his tax table without hesitation. Imagine Jesus saying, "Hey, guys, I'll see you in Capernaum. I'm organizing a group of men for a special mission. Come join Me when you can get away." No. His summons was urgent. "Come now!"

The words of the hymn "Just as I Am" express the expected response:

> Just as I am without one plea,
> But that Thy blood was shed for me;
> And that Thou bid me come to Thee,
> O Lamb of God, I come, I come.

Again from the Gospel of Luke,

> Now it happened as they journeyed on the road, that someone said to Him, "Lord, I will follow You wherever You go."
>
> And Jesus said to him, "Foxes have holes and birds of the air have nests, but the Son of Man has nowhere to lay His head." Then He said to another, "Follow Me."
>
> But he said, "Lord, let me first go and bury my father."
>
> Jesus said to him, "Let the dead bury their own dead, but you go and preach the kingdom of God."
>
> And another also said, "Lord, I will follow You, but let me first go and bid them farewell who are at my house."

But Jesus said to him, "No one, having put his hand to the plow, and looking back, is fit for the kingdom of God." (Luke 9:57–62 KJV)

I see nothing in the Gospels to indicate that the men in this story ever followed Him. How vital it is to embrace the gospel *at once*, to accept without delay Jesus' gracious invitation, and to follow the path that leads to life!

Jesus never accepted excuses for rejecting His call.

Luke recorded the following parable:

A man was giving a dinner, and he invited many; and at the dinner hour he sent his slave to say to those who had been invited, "Come; for everything is ready now." But they all alike began to make excuses.

The first one said to him, "I have bought a piece of land and I need to go out and look at it; please consider me excused."

Another one said, "I have bought five yoke of oxen, and I am going to try them out; please consider me excused."

Another one said, "I have married a wife, and for that reason I cannot come." (Luke 14:16–20)

The parable goes on to teach that there will always be room for those who will accept the Master's invitation to salvation, to sanctification, and to service. Jesus had no time for half-hearted, mediocre followers who were unwilling to do so on His terms. His requirements for discipleship are exacting. An important disciple-making principle can be stated here: *don't waste time on the half-hearted, wishy-washy, too quick candidate while so many others have yet to hear the call.*

Jesus never begged, pleaded, or called a person more than once.

I am not aware of any place in the Gospels where a person chose to follow Christ who had on some previous occasion rejected or declined the Savior's invitation. We must want to follow Jesus; it must be our will to do so. Jesus' call was simple, clear, and succinct—much different from those invitations to the altar that often employ everything akin to manipulation to get people down the aisle. It goes without saying that the Holy Spirit doesn't need help in drawing people to Jesus. This doesn't mean, however, that we ourselves should not plead with God for those who have not yet found the Savior.

Although Jesus gave most of His time and attention to the twelve, His general call to discipleship remained in force. Few, however, were willing to pay the price.

> As a result of this many of His disciples withdrew and were not walking with Him anymore. So Jesus said to the twelve, "You do not want to go away also, do you?" Simon Peter answered Him, "Lord, to whom shall we go? You have words of eternal life. We have believed and have come to know that You are the Holy One of God." (John 6:66–69)

When many were turning away from Jesus, His message to Peter was incisive. "Let them go! You follow Me." Time and again, through His preaching, teaching, and exhortation, Jesus repeated these conditions for discipleship. There is a cost involved in following Him. He wanted them, and He wants us to know it. While we do not see this emphasis in every word Jesus spoke, it is nevertheless hard to miss in reading the Gospels.

CHAPTER 2

THE COST OF DISCIPLESHIP

"Whoever does not carry his own cross and come after Me cannot be My disciple."

—Luke 14:27

A builder who does not count the cost before laying the foundation is humiliated as a disgraceful failure, yet an unfinished life is far more tragic than a rock foundation without a building.

Jesus warned the crowds:

> For which one of you, when he wants to build a tower, does not first sit down and calculate the cost to see if he has enough to complete it? Otherwise, when he has laid a foundation and is not able to finish, all who observe it begin to ridicule him, saying, "This man began to build and was not able to finish." Or what king, when he sets out to meet another king in battle, will not first sit down and consider whether he is strong enough with ten thousand men to encounter the one coming against him with twenty thousand? Or else, while the other is still far away, he sends a delegation and asks for terms of peace. (Luke 14:28–32)

William MacDonald, in *True Discipleship*, opens with the following:

> True Christianity is an all-out commitment to the Lord Jesus Christ. The Savior is not looking for men and

women who will give their spare evenings to Him—or their weekends—or their years of retirement. Rather He seeks those who will give Him first place in their lives. He looks today, as He has ever looked, not for crowds drifting aimlessly in His track, but for individual men and women whose undying allegiance will spring from their having recognized that He wants those who are prepared to follow the path of self-renunciation which He trod before them.

The Lord made stringent demands on those who would be His disciples—demands that are all but overlooked in this day of luxury living. Too often we look upon Christianity as an escape from hell and a guarantee of heaven. Beyond that, we feel that we have every right to enjoy the best that this life has to offer. We know that there are strong verses on discipleship in the Bible, but we have difficulty reconciling them with our own ideas of what Christianity should be."[1]

As discussed previously, the call to follow Jesus is associated with a cost—one that we cannot fail to see as we read the Gospels. It may mean forsaking one's job or vocation and giving up material possessions. It may involve a family separation. Following Jesus certainly means obedience and, as the Bible says, even persecution: "Indeed, all who desire to live godly in Christ Jesus will be persecuted" (2 Tim. 3:12). One of the greatest obstacles to following Jesus today is the stranglehold of materialism. The apostle John wrote,

Do not love the world or the things in the world. If anyone loves the world, the love of the Father is not in him. For all that is in the world, the lust of the flesh and the lust of the eyes and the boastful pride of life, is not from the Father, but is from the world. The world is passing away, and also its lusts; but the one who does the will of God lives forever. (1 John 2:15–17)

Again and again, Jesus taught this principle to His hearers:

> Do not worry then, saying, "What will we eat?" or "What will we drink?" or "What will we wear for clothing?" For the Gentiles eagerly seek all these things; for your heavenly Father knows that you need all these things. But seek first His kingdom and His righteousness, and all these things will be added to you. So do not worry about tomorrow; for tomorrow will care for itself. Each day has enough trouble of its own. (Matt. 6:31–34)

The following witty prayer expresses the problem of materialism and the good life today:

> Now I lay me down to sleep, I pray my house in Malibu to keep. I pray my stocks are on the rise, and that my analyst is wise; that all the wine I sip is white, and that my hot tub's watertight; that racquetball won't get too tough, that all my sushi's fresh enough. I pray my cordless phone still works, that my career won't lose its perks; my microwave won't radiate, my condo won't depreciate. I pray my health club doesn't close, and that my money market grows. If I go broke before I wake, I pray my Volvo they won't take. [Unknown source]

Consider now the following unconditional terms of discipleship, in Jesus' own words:

There must be a love for Christ that exceeds all other relationships.

"Now large crowds were going along with Him; and He turned and said to them, 'If anyone comes to Me, and does not hate his own father and mother and wife and children and brothers and sisters, yes, and even his own life, he cannot be My disciple'" (Luke 14:26). This troubling verse doesn't have to be as difficult to understand as some would make it. Jesus is simply comparing a person's love for Christ with that of his most beloved—his immediate family. When we consider all that Jesus said about the command to love, it will be clear that in this statement He was in no way lessening the importance of that obligation. When asked about the greatest commandment, He said, "'You shall love the Lord your God with all your heart, soul, mind, and strength;' and the second is like unto it, 'You shall love your neighbor as yourself'" (Mark 10:42–43). (See chapter 3, "The Great Commandment.")

There must be wholehearted, unswerving devotion to Christ.

Jesus issued this charge to those who would follow Him: "Whoever does not carry his own cross and come after Me cannot be My disciple" (Luke 14:27). The cross is not some physical infirmity or mental anguish but a pathway that may involve reproach, suffering, loneliness, and even death, which a person voluntarily chooses for Christ's sake. Not all believers bear the cross; it is possible to avoid it by living a nominal (in name only) Christian life. But if we determine to be all out for Christ, we will experience the same kind of satanic oppression that the Son of God knew.

To be unswervingly devoted to Christ is to abide in Him. Andrew Murray writes about the blessedness of such a life:

> If, in our orthodox churches, the abiding in Christ, the living union with Him, the experience of His daily and hourly presence and keeping, were preached with the same distinctness and urgency as His atonement and pardon through His blood, I am confident that many would be found to accept with gladness the invitation to such a life, and that its influence would be manifest in their experience of the purity and power, the love and the joy, the fruit-bearing, all of the blessedness which the Savior connected with the abiding in Him.[2]

What genuine Christian could really understand this great truth and refuse it? In contemporary speech, one might say, "Give it everything you've got—hold nothing back." As the church father St. Augustine said, "Jesus Christ is not valued at all until He is valued above all."

There must be a forsaking of all one has.

"So then, none of you can be My disciple who does not give up all his own possessions" (Luke 14:33.)

> This is perhaps the most unpopular of all Christ's terms of discipleship, and may well prove to be the most unpopular verse in the Bible. Clever theologians can give you a thousand reasons why it does not mean what it says, but simple disciples drink it down eagerly, assuming that the Lord Jesus knew what He was saying. Such a person, in seeking first the kingdom of God and His righteousness, does not want to waste his life accumulating riches that will fall into the devil's hands when Christ returns for His saints. He wants to obey the Lord's injunction against laying up treasure on earth. In forsaking all, he offers what he cannot keep anyway, and what he has ceased to love.[3]

Martyred missionary Jim Elliot made this classic statement: "He is no fool who gives up what he cannot keep to gain what he cannot lose." A true disciple, in accordance with this command, will hold everything he owns in open hands, having deeded ownership to God. He is prepared to let it go as God leads him.

There must be a consistent intake and obedience to the Word of God.

"So Jesus was saying to those Jews who had believed Him, 'If you continue in My word, then you are truly disciples of Mine; and you will know the truth, and the truth will make you free'" (John 8:31–32).

Christ comes to us in the written Word, the Bible, brought home to our souls by the Holy Spirit. As we feed upon the words of scripture, we are feeding upon the living Christ. God has promised great blessings to those who seek Him, trust Him, and obey His Word. Spiritual filling and growth come from an intimate relationship with God. From this close communion with God, we derive strength and guidance for living and for facing the trials and adversities of life. From the Bible, we gain knowledge and understanding of what God requires of us as followers of Jesus Christ. God's Word guides us in making wise decisions. He also promises to bless us when we learn and obey His Word. Let's not overlook the sheer joy of communing with Him daily through reading and meditating upon His Word.

There must be unconditional love for others.

Near the end of His earthly life, Jesus told His disciples, "By this all men will know that you are My disciples, if you have love for one another" (John 13:35). The badge of Christian discipleship is not a cross worn around the neck or some distinctive type of clothing. Anyone can profess discipleship by these means. The true mark of a Christian is love for his fellow Christians. This requires divine power, and this power is only given to those indwelt by the Spirit. Love is the antithesis of selfishness. Love is the preeminent virtue produced by Christianity. The whole law is summed up in love, not in the sense of rendering all other requirements as inconsequential but in the sense that love is fundamental, expresses the spirit of all others, and with enlightenment will lead to the observance of all others.

Accordingly, love is declared to be the chief test of Christian discipleship. It is the highest motive of moral actions. Without this, all others fall short of furnishing the true stimulus of Christian living. As all sin roots itself in selfishness, so all virtue springs out of love, and yet the love that is presented in the New Testament as the mainspring of holy living is grateful love.

There must be an ongoing pattern of spiritual fruitfulness.

Fruitfulness is used in two ways in John 15. Jesus said, "My Father is glorified by this, *that you bear much fruit*, and so prove to be My disciples … You did not choose Me but I chose you, and appointed you *that you would go and bear fruit*, and that your fruit would remain, so that whatever you ask of the Father in my name He may give to you" (John 15:8, 16).

Verse 8 refers to the fruit of the Spirit, the natural expression in a Christian's life of certain Spirit-produced qualities: "But the fruit of the Spirit is love, joy, peace, patience, kindness, goodness, faithfulness, gentleness, self-control" (Gal. 5:22–23). Bearing fruit (verse 8) also includes everything in a believer's life resulting from his or her obedience to Jesus' commands, as found in the New Testament. In verse 16, *fruit* means lives impacted by the Gospel: people saved, instructed, and trained in Christian living and service and in other ways changed as a result of a personal encounter with Jesus Christ. If we are true disciples, we will bear both kinds of fruit continually throughout our lives.

There can be no turning back.

Jesus said, "No one, having put his hand to the plow, and looking back, is fit for the kingdom of God" (Luke 9:62). In 1519, Spanish conquistador Hernando Cortez landed in Mexico on the shores of the Yucatan with six hundred men and prepared for battle with the formidable native population. Knowing the terror of his men, the captain ordered that the boats be burnt on the shore so that there was no retreat. He knew that while there was the option for escape, his men would only half-heartedly fight, expecting the call to withdraw to come at any moment. By burning the boats, he steadied the resolve of his men and commanded their full commitment to the battle. They went on to defeat their enemy and claim the substantial riches of the Aztecs.

In a similar story, when Julius Caesar landed on the shores of Britain with his Roman legions, he took a bold and decisive step to ensure the success of his military venture. Ordering his men to march to the edge of the Cliffs of Dover, he commanded them to look down at the water below. To their amazement, they saw every ship in which they had crossed the channel engulfed in flames. Caesar had deliberately cut off any possibility of retreat. Now that his soldiers were unable to return to the continent, there was nothing left for them to do but to advance and conquer! And that is exactly what they did.

A follower of Jesus Christ must go where He leads, whether to a next-door neighbor or a foreign mission field. Keith Parks, former president of the Southern Baptist Foreign Mission Board, was the guest speaker at a chapel service at the Southern Baptist Theological Seminary in Louisville, Kentucky. As a seminary student, I attended the service that morning. Parks' powerful message was followed by an outpouring of the Holy Spirit such as I have rarely seen in a worship service—before or since. What stood out to me the most, however, was his account of an interview he had conducted with a prospective missionary candidate. The young man asked this question regarding the mission for which he was being considered: "But will it be safe?" While I do not recall the speaker's exact words, he went on to make it abundantly and emphatically clear that that question need not be asked if we are moving in the will of God—following His call to service. We are safer in God's will anywhere in the world than outside God's will in our own homes. A true disciple must have a mindset that simply will not allow him to turn back once he has answered Jesus' call.

SECTION 2

Discipleship Inspired

CHAPTER 3

MOTIVATION FOR DISCIPLE-MAKING

"If you love Me, you will keep My commandments."
—John 14:15

One of my duties as a staff officer in the army was to process applications for hardship discharges and conscientious objector status. My boss led me to some shelves that contained a dozen or more large three-ring binders.

"These are the Department of Defense Regulations," he said, pointing to one of the binders. He pointed to another one and said, "These are the Department of the Army Regulations." Then he showed me the Fort Leonard Wood Regulations, the US Army Training Center Regulations, the Brigade Regulations, and some other procedures and protocols.

"Just familiarize yourself with all of these, and you'll have no problem doing this job. When the applications come through, check the regulations, write your reports, and send them up through channels."

What if all those regulations could have been condensed into just a few simple guidelines, or better yet, into a single command?

In a sense, this is exactly what Jesus did. He took all of the laws and commandments that God had given the Jews and combined them into one supreme command.

The Great Commandment

> "The first of all the commandments is: 'Hear, O Israel, the Lord our God, the Lord is one. And you shall love the Lord your God with all your heart, with all your soul, with all your mind, and with all your strength.'" (Mark 12:28)

> "And the second, like it, is this: 'You shall love your neighbor as yourself.' There is no other commandment greater than these." (Mark 12:31)

Stated simply, Jesus said, "Love God and love your neighbor." The apostle Paul simplified it even more: "For all the law is fulfilled in one word, even in this: 'You shall love your neighbor as yourself'" (Gal. 5:14). He could say this because he understood that in order to truly love God, we must also love our neighbor; that genuine love for our neighbor is evidence of our love for God. The essential question is this: "What does it mean to love our neighbor?" If this is what we have to do to meet God's requirements, then it is imperative that we too understand what "loving our neighbor" is about.

Love meets needs in people's lives. Jesus told His disciples, "Do you not say, 'Four months more and then the harvest'? I tell you, open your eyes and look at the fields! They are ripe for harvest" (John 4:35). We observe an unending array of human needs: a man with a terminal illness; a woman suffering the pain of divorce or grieving over the death of a loved one; a man who has lost his job and is facing serious financial difficulties; a person living with discouragement or depression; a couple dealing with a problem teenager; an elderly woman with failing health and a fear of death; an accident victim living with pain; a single person trapped in loneliness; and people who just feel unloved or unappreciated.

God uses believers as His representatives, or agents, in sharing His love and compassion. People need a listening ear and words of kindness from someone who genuinely cares about them. Within every person is a desire to be wanted, needed, and fulfilled. Most important, though, is the need to know and experience the love of God and His power to change their lives. This comes only through a personal relationship with Jesus Christ.

Years ago, I traveled to Philadelphia, Pennsylvania, to attend an advanced optometry course. I was living in Louisville and wanted to ride a train, but there were no longer any trains running between Louisville and Philadelphia. I had to ride a bus to Indianapolis in order to catch a train to Philadelphia. Where there is no track, there can be no train. A train requires a track to go anywhere.

Similarly, love flows from one person to another through relationships, which provide opportunities to help people. Genuine friendliness, listening to people's problems and concerns, displaying a sincere interest in them, and performing acts of kindness can lead to genuine, long-lasting relationships.

Christians are called to love believers and unbelievers alike. In the case of unbelievers, the primary goal should be to gain opportunities to share Christ. What may begin with a casual conversation in the workplace could lead to a discussion in the coffee shop about the Bible or sharing a word of testimony on the golf course. An intermediate goal should be to gain a person's confidence in order to engage him or her with the Gospel. Sometimes this can take place very quickly. For example, a person receiving medical care from a missionary doctor may willingly listen to the message of Christ or accept a Gospel tract. But apart from such ready-made situations, time and effort may be required for the kind of relationships through which we can really love people and share the Gospel.

Relationships are also helpful in demonstrating love to our brothers and sisters in Christ. Paul exhorted the Thessalonians to comfort and edify one another, to uphold the weak, to rejoice and pray for one another, and much more (1 Thess. 5:11–14). This is Christian love. Someone asked how he could know for certain that he is loving people in this way? A wise counselor responded, "People will beat a path to your door and your phone will not stop ringing when you genuinely love and care for them. They will witness and experience the love of God through you."

Jesus said, "Do not work for the food which perishes, but for the food which endures to eternal life, which the Son of Man will give to you, for on Him God, the Father, has set His seal" (John 6:27). There are only two things that last forever: the Word of God and the souls of people. Loving God and loving people go together. We must impact people with the Gospel. What, then, is the Great Commandment? It is to serve people as God gives us opportunities, to influence unbelievers toward salvation, and to encourage and assist fellow Christians in the path to spiritual maturity.

The Great Commission

"Go therefore and make disciples of all the nations, baptizing them in the name of the Father and the Son and the Holy Spirit, teaching them to observe all that I commanded you;and lo, I am with you always, even to the end of the age." (Matt. 28:19–20)

Disciple-making begins with the Great Commission, Jesus' final words to His disciples. In order to understand the Great Commission, let's consider an event that took place in 1776 during the American Revolution. Paul Revere's commanding officer called him in and said, "Paul, I want you to go through all the towns and villages and shout, 'The British are coming,' waking up all who are asleep and stopping at all the taverns where people might be gathered."

Now what was his command? Was it to go through the towns and villages? Yes. Was it to stop by the taverns where people might be found? Sure. Was his command to wake people up? Of course it was. But what was his primary command—the real purpose of his mission? What was Paul Revere sent to do? You guessed it. He was sent to shout, to cry as loud as he could, "The British are coming!"

What are we commissioned to do? We are commissioned to make disciples: "Going therefore, make disciples—baptizing and teaching." The process involves baptizing and teaching, but the command is to make disciples. I believe that this began with God's command to Adam: "Be fruitful and multiply" (Gen. 1:28). He said it again when Noah and his family came off of the ark. Many years later, God promised Abraham, "I will make you exceedingly fruitful; and I will make nations of you" (Gen. 17:6). God is saying, "I want more just like you. I want every one of you to reproduce and multiply your life."

The Great Commission begins with evangelism, sharing the Gospel with the goal of winning people to Jesus Christ. We can help carry out this command whether we are on some foreign mission field or in our regular place of work. We are involved in the work of evangelism any time we witness for Christ. But the Great Commission does not stop with evangelism—it includes helping new believers grow toward spiritual maturity through the process of disciple-making.

What is a disciple of Jesus Christ, and what does it mean to be a disciple-maker? Christopher Adsit, in his book *Disciple-Making*, offers the following definitions:

> A disciple of Jesus Christ is one who is ever learning from Him and, though use and practice, is growing in his commitment to a Christian lifestyle. To make disciples is to nurture the spiritually new born and immature, to teach them to feed themselves from the Word of God; to model obedient Christian life for them; and train them to reproduce these things in the life of another.[1]

So a true disciple is much more than a person who has been born again, one merely converted to Christianity, but a person committed to following Jesus. Jesus said, "I will make you fishers of men." Jesus made the first disciples. In the Great Commission, He did not say "Go be disciples"—the twelve were already disciples—but "Go make disciples." He had trained them for the task; now He was sending them out.

In Exodus, we read about Moses leading the Israelites out of Egypt after four hundred years of slavery. Early in their journey, Moses ascended Mount Sinai to receive the Ten Commandments. During the forty days he was on the mountain, the people grew restless and fell into idolatry. They built and worshiped a golden calf. Moses saw that the people were out of control—for Aaron had let them get out of control to become a derision among their enemies (Exod. 32:25).

There is a city in South America that conducts an annual carnival, where for one day each year, anything goes. For that one day, the people just do whatever they want. They fill the streets of the city and celebrate, running wild, without restraint. The word *carnival* comes from the word *carnal*, which refers to the flesh. This seems to describe much of the world today—unrestrained, out of control, running wild.

The Bible says, "Now the boy Samuel was ministering to the LORD before Eli. And word from the LORD was rare in those days, visions were infrequent" (1 Sam. 3:1). In other words, the people of Israel rarely heard from God. The same word is used for *vision* in Proverbs 29:18. "Where there is no vision, the people are unrestrained." The greatest challenge that we face as evangelical, mission-minded Christians is this: the world is in need of the Gospel of Jesus Christ. Christ is the only hope for the lost and dying masses. As with the Great Commandment, the Great Commission is about giving ourselves to people, that they might turn to God for salvation.

The Great Commitment

"If anyone desires to come after Me, let him deny himself, and take up his cross, and follow Me." *(*Matthew 16:24*)*

Jesus fed five thousand men, plus women and children, before preaching His "Bread of Life" sermon. His words became so difficult to accept that "many of His disciples went back and walked with Him no more. Then Jesus said to the twelve, 'You do not want to go away also, do you?' Simon Peter answered Him, 'Lord, to whom shall we go? You have words of eternal life. We have believed and have come to know that You are the Holy One of God'" (John 6:66–68).

Our commitment to Jesus Christ must not be too spontaneous, emotional, or half-hearted:

- "Lord, I will follow You wherever You go, but first let me graduate from college."
- "Lord, I will follow You wherever You go, but first let me graduate from optometry school."
- "Lord, I will follow You wherever You go, but first let me pass my board exams; let me get my practice established and my career underway."
- "Lord, I will follow You wherever You go, but first let me get out of debt."

We cannot follow Christ on our own terms but by wholehearted, unconditional commitment to Him as the Lord of our lives. Jesus was speaking about this Great Commitment when He said, "If anyone wishes to come after Me, he must deny himself, and take up his cross and follow Me" (Matt. 16:24); likewise Paul, when he wrote, "I have been crucified with Christ; and it is no longer I who live, but Christ lives in me; and the life which I now live in the flesh I live by faith in the Son of God, who loved me and gave Himself up for me"(Gal. 2:20).

The following is from an article by Clayton Bell:

> A number of years ago Norman Cousins wrote an editorial in Saturday Review in which he reported a conversation he had on a trip in India. He was talking with a Hindu priest named Satis Prasad. The man said he wanted to come to our country to work as a missionary among the Americans.
>
> Cousins assumed that he meant that he wanted to convert Americans to the Hindu religion, but when asked, Satis Prasad said, "Oh no, I would like to convert them to the Christian religion. Christianity cannot survive in the abstract. It needs not membership, but believers. The people of your country may claim they believe in Christianity, but from what I read at this distance, Christianity is more a custom than anything else. I would ask that either you accept the teachings of Jesus in your everyday life and in your affairs as a nation, or stop invoking His name as sanction for everything you do. I want to help save Christianity for the Christian." [2]

Jehu said, "Come with me and see my zeal for the LORD" (2 Kings 10:16). As a new Christian, I was enthusiastic about sharing my newly discovered faith in Jesus Christ. My goal at that time was to verbally witness to each of the twenty students in my optometry class. (Some were already Christians.) Later, I realized that I had set my sights too short; my goal should have been to witness to every student in the school.

Once, after I had spoken at a nearby church, my photograph and an article about the event appeared in a local newspaper. The next morning, my clinical instructor said wryly, "Segree, I didn't know that you were a man of the cloth." I did not consider myself a man of the cloth, but the occasion did give me an opportunity to witness. Later, I came to understand that God's plan is for *every believer* to present a positive witness for Jesus Christ in the workplace.

May we never have to say, "God, what have I done with my life? I have devoted my life to the wrong things; the pursuit of wealth, materialism, pleasure, power, and the like." Instead, may we be led by these words of

Jesus: "Do not work for the food which perishes, but for the food which endures to eternal life" (John 6:27).

God spoke through the prophet Isaiah: "Do not fear, for I have redeemed you; I have called you by name; you are Mine … Since you are precious in My sight, Since you are honored and I love you, I will give other men in your place and other peoples in exchange for your life" (Isa. 43:1, 4). This is a promise every believer can claim: "God, give people for my life. Let me invest in people. Let me become a disciple-maker." This is the spirit of the Great Commandment, the Great Commission, and the Great Commitment.

SECTION 3

Discipleship Imparted

CHAPTER 4

A PERSONAL MINISTRY

"The things you have learned and received and heard and seen in me, practice these things, and the God of peace will be with you."

—Philippians 4:9

When making disciples, we must look to Jesus as our ultimate teacher, model, and guide. There is no shortcut or substitute for one person helping another to grow in his relationship to Christ. Only a disciple can make a disciple. A person cannot lead someone where he himself has not been.

Oswald Chambers writes about making disciples:

> Our work is not to save souls, but to disciple them. Salvation and sanctification are the work of God's sovereign grace, and our work as His disciples is to disciple others' lives until they are totally yielded to God. One life totally devoted to God is of more value to Him than one hundred lives which have been simply awakened to His Spirit. As workers for God, we must reproduce our own kind spiritually, and those lives will be God's testimony to us as His workers. God brings us up to a standard of life through His grace, and we are responsible for reproducing that same standard in others.[1]

Yet we must not miss the fact that disciple-making begins with evangelism. If we work only with Christians in our disciple-making ministry, then the net gain to the kingdom of God is zero. Aggressive evangelism is the mark of the committed disciple, and it is primarily from the fruit of this evangelism that he discovers the candidate for disciple-making.

Men and women were Jesus' method of making disciples. In three years, He preached and ministered to the masses, sent out seventy followers, and trained and sent out twelve apostles. (Yet even one of these dropped out.) He devoted extra time and attention to three: Peter, James, and John. Whatever a disciple-maker is, Jesus was; whatever a disciple is, the twelve were. The worldwide spread of genuine Christianity through the centuries is a result of those first disciples becoming disciple-makers themselves.

There is often a missing emphasis upon *doing* in Bible teaching, and a missing emphasis upon *training* in the life of a growing Christian. There must be an emphasis upon the *how-to* of making disciples. Jesus taught His disciples many things, but He never taught hearing and knowing without doing. "You know these things. Blessed are you if you do them" (John 13:17).

Jesus trained His men through constant association, equipped them for their mission, and sent them out to win the world. His life, teaching, and methods are the starting point and the key to our understanding of our role as disciple-makers. One must not only look to Jesus but be with Him and strive to be like Him.

In *The Master Plan of Evangelism*, Robert Coleman says,

> As one reads through the Gospel accounts, it becomes evident that Jesus spent more and more time with His disciples as He approached His final days. The time which He invested in these few disciples was so much more in comparison to that given to others that it can only be regarded as a deliberate strategy. He actually spent more time with His disciples than with everybody else in the world put together. He ate with them, slept with them, and talked with them for the most part of His active ministry. They walked together along the lonely roads; they visited together in the crowded cities; they sailed and fished together on the Sea of Galilee; they prayed together in the deserts and in the mountains; and they worshiped together in the synagogues and in the Temple.[2]

Where do we find our candidates for disciple-making? Wherever there are people, there is an opportunity for evangelism and disciple-making.

Simply stated, anyone who is willing to respond to our efforts is a potential disciple. This may include Christians who are still spiritual infants. Churches are filled with such people. We must be discerning, praying for the Holy Spirit to show us those who are willing to follow.

↶↷

Henry Ford had been trying to increase his automobile factories' productivity for years. On December 1, 1913, he installed the first moving assembly line for the mass production of an entire automobile. (Mass production began during the Industrial Revolution but took a great leap forward with the innovation of the assembly line, a conveyor that moved the product from one workman to another, with each individual adding his or her specialty part to the growing whole.) Ford's innovation reduced the time it took to build a car from more than twelve hours to one hour and thirty-three minutes.

Unfortunately, this is exactly the approach many Christian ministries take. Get as many as we can into the auditorium or in front of the television on Sunday morning; preach to them and hope that somehow in some way some disciples will emerge. While a few self-motivated, Spirit-led individuals may come forth under such circumstances, this clearly is not the model for disciple-making taught and practiced by Jesus and the apostles. While it is important that this ministry be understood within the overall disciple-making task of the local church, disciple-making is at its best an individual, personal ministry—one person pouring his/her life into that of another. (See appendix A, "The Process of Disciple-Making.")

LeRoy Eims addresses this in *The Lost Art of Disciple-Making*:

> The ministry is to be carried on by people, not programs.
> It is to be carried out by someone and not by some thing.
> Disciples cannot be mass produced. We cannot drop people
> into a "program" and see disciples emerge at the end of
> the production line. It takes time to make disciples. It takes
> individual, personal attention. It takes hours of prayer for
> them. It takes patience and understanding to teach them
> how to get into the Word of God for themselves, how to
> feed and nourish their souls, and by the power of the Holy

Spirit how to apply the Word to their lives. And it takes being an example to them of all of the above.[3]

Walt Henrichsen, in *Disciples Are Made, Not Born*, writes,

> For the sake of simplicity, let me suggest that development can be categorized into three areas: teaching, training, and building. I will define teaching as the imparting of knowledge, training as the imparting of skill, and building as the imparting of character. The development of our disciple must include all three—teaching, training, and building.[4]

Disciple-making is a lifelong process, the first step being that of helping a new convert. The initial step in disciple-making is known as *follow-up*. Scott Morton provides the following story:

> In the 1950's Billy Graham came to Dawson Trotman and explained that in the great revivals of history, there was never much of a "follow-up" program to help new believers grow. He asked for Dawson's help.
> But Dawson told Billy he was too busy working with sailors and launching "The Navigators." "You'll have to get someone else," he said.
> Before the words were out of Dawson's mouth, the 6'2" Graham grabbed the 5'6" Trotman by the shoulders and said, "Who else? Who's been majoring in this?"
> It was true that Dawson and The Navigators had been majoring in follow-up. So Trotman and some of his meager staff worked with the Graham organization from 1949 to 1954, pioneering the follow-up methods and materials still used by the Graham team. Now, fifty years later, the term "follow-up" is common among Christian leaders.[5]

New Christians who are not properly followed up after conversion run the risk of remaining spiritual infants for the rest of their lives. Paul wrote about follow-up regarding the church in Thessalonica: "But we proved to be gentle among you, as a nursing mother tenderly cares for her own children. Having so fond an affection for you, we were well-pleased to impart to you not only the gospel of God but also our own lives, because you had become very dear to us" (1 Thess. 2:7–8).

Would a young man who had just joined the football team be sent onto the field with no training, physical conditioning, or knowledge of the rules? Would an aspiring musician be allowed to perform publicly without first mastering the fundamentals of the instrument? Would a soldier be sent into battle without completing basic training? Of course not, yet new believers are often chosen to occupy places of ministry in the church without first being followed-up (i.e., established in the fundamentals of the faith). It is equally unacceptable (even inexcusable) for a new or spiritually immature Christian to be welcomed into the church and merely encouraged to attend services once or twice a week and nothing more. The writer of Hebrews addressed the problem resulting from inadequate follow-up and disciple-making in the early churches:

> For though by this time you ought to be teachers, you have need again for someone to teach you the elementary principles of the oracles of God, and you have come to need milk and not solid food. For everyone who partakes only of milk is not accustomed to the word of righteousness, for he is an infant. But solid food is for the mature, who because of practice have their senses trained to discern good and evil. (Heb. 5:12–14)

Peter said it this way: "Like newborn babies, long for the pure milk of the word, so that by it you may grow in respect to salvation, if you have tasted the kindness of the Lord" (1 Peter 2:2). The needs of a new Christian are very much like those of a newborn baby: love, food, and protection. After assurance of salvation, he needs love and acceptance by the body of Christ. He must be fed spiritually and taught how to feed himself from the Word of God. He must be protected from whatever would harm him but especially from Satan's efforts to hinder his Christian growth.

Suppose a mother wants to train her baby to eat. Would she simply give the child a jar of food, a can opener, and a spoon? Would she have her baby watch a video about how to eat? That's absurd. She would feed the baby herself and gradually teach him how to hold the spoon, dip the food, and bring it to his mouth. As parents, we provide our children everything they need in order to grow and develop normally. As disciple-makers, we have an equal responsibility to provide our spiritual offspring everything they need for normal growth and development.

We cannot assume that the average Christian can simply read a book or complete a workbook on the subject of discipleship and/or disciple-making and go on to effectively lead another through the process. One-on-one instruction, interaction, and encouragement are needed. For this reason, we should refrain from simply giving a prospective disciple something to read and fill out. Just as there is no shortcut to properly caring for a newborn baby, there is no shortcut to spiritual nurturing of a new convert or growing Christian. Unless these principles are thoroughly understood and incorporated into the life of the believer, he will not be able to successfully pass them on to another, thus terminating the process of spiritual reproduction.

The one who is seeking salvation—not yet a true believer—must not be allowed to come to the threshold of the kingdom of God and then be lost for lack of sufficient nurturing and nourishment. You must direct or accompany him to a church where the Bible is preached faithfully and to a Sunday school class or group Bible study. Pray for him daily and pray with him as you have opportunity.

As disciple-makers, we must be pacesetters; we must set the proper example for our disciples. The apostle Paul developed good habits in the Word, prayer, teaching, preaching, working, and witnessing. No wonder he could say to his followers, "The things you have learned and received and heard and seen in me, practice these things, and the God of peace will be with you" (Phil. 4:9).

CHAPTER 5

A FRUITFUL MINISTRY

"I chose you, and appointed you that you would go and
bear fruit, that your fruit would remain, so that whatever
you ask of the Father in My name He may give to you."

—John 15:16

Our Ultimate Goal: Spiritual Reproduction and Multiplication

*Multiplication is the key to reaching the greatest number of people in the most
effective way in the shortest period of time.*

In a general sense, reproduction is one of the most important concepts in
biology. It means "making a copy, a likeness," and thereby providing for the
continued existence of species. To multiply means to increase in number
by reproduction. When something is multiplied, it is reproduced over and
over again in like form. In the natural world, we reproduce ourselves by
having children; we multiply physically. Similarly, we multiply spiritually
by producing spiritual offspring.

When Jesus told His disciples, "Go and make disciples of all nations,"
He set into motion His plan for world evangelism—the process of spiritual
multiplication. The first disciples and the early church were obedient to
that command, and as a result, the body of Christ experienced phenomenal
growth.

The vision of spiritual multiplication is largely absent in churches today, yet it is the key to the fulfillment of the Great Commission. Multiplication should take place at both the individual and corporate levels, as in the New Testament. Individual disciples reproduced one by one, while churches did so through the planting of new churches. We may not be called (or be able) to start new churches, but as individual believers, we can bear lasting fruit by making disciples—one by one.

In *The Timothy Principle,* Roy Robertson writes about spiritual reproduction:

> My thesis is that God's basic plan for perpetuating life, both physical and spiritual, is through reproduction. There are two key principles about reproduction. First, only life can produce life. This is obvious in the physical realm. I proposed to my wife on top of Victoria Peak, overlooking the fascinating harbor of Hong Kong. Later we were married at the beautiful mountain estate of Glen Eyrie, in Colorado Springs. Eventually we returned overseas. One of our children was born in Colorado and our twins were born in Singapore. Our days of physically producing children are now past, but the seed of life has been passed on to our offspring. We have grandchildren, and there will probably be many more. Even after we die, our children and grandchildren will continue to produce offspring, and their children will produce even more children. The process of physical life will thus go on and on.
>
> Spiritual life begins through Jesus Christ. He is the Life that brings man back from spiritual death (John 11:25; 14:6). When you believe in Christ, the Spirit of God is implanted in your heart. This Spirit confirms your salvation to your own heart and to the hearts of others. Spiritual life begins in Christ and is then passed on to others through the Christian, who possesses spiritual life.
>
> It is our responsibility to pass on this spiritual life to others. They receive Christ through faith in the Word. But how can people believe unless we tell them about Jesus? God's plan reveals that mere human beings on earth, not the angels of heaven, are the means of bringing other people to Christ.

As noted previously, all living beings reproduce after
their own kind: animals, plants—everything. In the same
way, God's plan for evangelizing the world is through
spiritual reproduction. Every born-again Christian has
the wonderful privilege and duty of bringing spiritual life
to others. Spiritual life is transmitted through *us*, people
who are spiritually alive! The eternal, incorruptible seed
of life everlasting is in you and me.[1]

An example of spiritual reproduction can be seen in Paul's first epistle
to the Corinthians: "Therefore I urge you, imitate me. For this reason I
have sent Timothy to you, who is my beloved and faithful son in the Lord,
who will remind you of my ways in Christ, as I teach everywhere in every
church" (1 Cor. 4:16–17).Paul could make the case with confidence that
the Corinthians could be like Him by following Timothy's example. We
reproduce after our own kind—both physically and spiritually.

What is the goal of one-to-one ministry? Is it to reach the second
spiritual generation? While this is where it must begin, the process is cut
short unless our disciples are faithfully reaching and making disciples of
the people in their own world, the third spiritual generation. This will take
longer than an eight-week discipleship course or small group Bible study.
In order to be effective in spiritual reproduction, we must understand and
have a vision for it. Here are two biblical examples of this principle:

> Jesus prayed for His disciples the night before he was
> crucified: "I ask on their behalf; I do not ask on behalf of
> the world, but of those whom You have given Me for they
> are Yours ... I do not ask on behalf of these alone, but for
> those also who believe in Me through their word" (John
> 17:9, 20).

In verse 9,Jesus is praying for the disciples whom God had given
Him—the twelve and perhaps a few others. Then in verse 20,He prays for
those who became believers through the ministry of the twelve—the third
generation. He fully expects His disciples to take the gospel to others. His
goal is bigger than just the twelve.

The apostle Paul had not only the third but also the fourth generation
in mind when he wrote to Timothy, "And the things that you have heard

from me among many witnesses, commit these to faithful men who will be able to teach others also" (2 Tim. 2:2).

Multiplication has been labeled the missing element in modern church growth. The worldwide spread of Christianity resulted from Christians passing it on to successive generations, who then passed it on to others. "But the word of the Lord continued to grow and to be multiplied" (Acts 12:24). Consider the difference between addition and multiplication: If a gifted pastor or evangelist could lead one hundred people to Christ every year, in twenty years, he would have won two thousand souls. But if he were to spend one year training a disciple to reproduce his life, and then each of them trained another in the following year, continuing the multiplication process for twenty years, the number would be an astronomical 1,048,576. While this is only theoretical (many will never reproduce, thereby stopping the process in their line), it does show the power of multiplication.

To summarize and emphasize the thesis of this section, I have included the following lengthy quote from Robert Coleman's *The Master Plan of Evangelism*:

> Here finally is where we must all must evaluate the contribution that our life and witness is making to the supreme purpose of him who is the Savior of the world. Are those who have followed us to Christ now leading others to him and teaching them to make disciples like ourselves? Note, it is not enough to rescue the perishing, though this is imperative; nor is it sufficient to build up newborn babes in the faith of Christ, although this too is necessary if the firstfruit is to endure; in fact, it is not sufficient to get them out winning souls, as commendable as this work may be. What really counts in the ultimate perpetuation of our work is the faithfulness with which our converts go out and make leaders out of their converts, not simply more followers. Surely we want to win our generation for Christ, and to do it now, but this is not enough. Our work is never finished until it has assured us its continuation in the lives of those redeemed by the Evangel.
>
> The test of any work of evangelism thus is not what is seen at the moment, or in the conference report, but

in the effectiveness with which the work continues in the next generation. Similarly the criteria on which a church should measure its success is not how many new names are added to the roll nor how much the budget is increased, but rather how many Christians are actively winning souls and training them to win the multitudes. The ultimate extent of our witness is what matters, and for this reason values can be measured only by eternity.

Is it not time that we all looked again at our lives and ministries from this perspective? As Dawson Trotman[2] would say, "Where are our men? What are they doing for God?"

Consider what it would mean to the future of the church if we had only one true disciple now to show for our labors? Would not this immediately double our influence? And suppose that we made another like ourself, even as the first succeeded in the same way. Would not this multiply our life four times over? Theoretically, at least, in this manner of multiplication, our ministry alone would soon reach multitudes with the gospel. That is, if that person we had called a disciple truly followed in the steps of the Master.[3]

A Long-Term Commitment

Disciple-making is not a sprint but a marathon. Adoniram Judson sweated out Burma's heat for eighteen years without a furlough, six years without a convert. Enduring torture and imprisonment, he admitted that he never saw a ship sail without wanting to jump on board and go home. When his wife's health broke, he put her on a homebound vessel in the knowledge that he would not see her again for two full years.

He confided to his diary: "If only we could find some quiet resting place on earth where we could spend the rest of our days in peace." But he steadied himself with this remarkable postscript: "Life is short. Millions of Burmese are perishing. I am almost the only person on earth who has attained their language to communicate salvation." Judson was a man who fulfilled his long-term commitment, persevered in his labor, and finished strong.[4]

A missionary society wrote to David Livingstone and asked, "Have you found a good road to where you are? If so, we want to know how to send other men to join you."

Livingstone wrote back, "If you have men who will come only if they know there is a good road, I don't want them. I want men who will come if there is no road at all" (source unknown).[5]

Jesus never called a person more than once, never begged anyone to follow Him, never accepted excuses, and never wasted time with the half-hearted and half-committed. He always attached a cost to following Him, and relatively few were willing to pay it. (See chapter 2, "The Cost of Discipleship.") There is an even greater cost to making disciples. George Sanchez, a member of the Navigators staff, once said this to a gathering of mostly young people at a conference I attended: "You must be willing to commit at least eighteen years of your life to each child you plan to bring into the world." You most likely will never commit *that much* time to a person in a disciple-making ministry but you must commit a significant amount.

In the case of every disciple-making relationship that Alma (my wife) and I have had over the past forty years, it has always been the disciple or trainee—neither of us—who ended it, for one reason or another. A good mindset for a disciple-maker is never to give up on a person who shows the potential for becoming a true disciple of Jesus Christ and who is willing to continue. As your disciple grows and no longer requires much of your time, continue to be available as a consultant and encourager. We are called to run the race with enthusiasm and vigor. Always keep in mind that, like the Christian life itself, disciple-making is not a sprint but a marathon.

Jesus said to His disciples, "You did not choose Me but I chose you, and appointed you that you would go and bear fruit, and that your fruit would remain, so that whatever you ask of the Father in My name He may give to you" (John 15:16). These words are especially relevant to us who are Great Commission (evangelical) Christians. Whether at home or on the foreign mission field, nothing we do in the area of evangelical missions will mean much if there are no lasting results. It is therefore imperative that we conserve the fruits of evangelism—making disciples and thereby raising up foundations for spiritual generations.

Theoretically (ideally), a new covert will progress through several stages of spiritual development during his period of growth. These stages may be somewhat arbitrary regarding their boundaries (we may drive from one state to another without seeing a boundary marker): convert, growing Christian, established disciple, disciple-maker, and maker of disciple-makers. There will be indicators, for example, that a person is a growing Christian, but when do we call him an established disciple? The point I am making is that our ministry to any one person will likely cover only a part of his spiritual journey. We may work with him for only a few weeks or a few months but enough, perhaps, to call him an established disciple, though hardly enough for him to become a disciple-maker. It is as the apostle Paul wrote the Corinthians:

> What then is Apollos? And what is Paul? Servants through whom you believed, even as the Lord gave opportunity to each one. I planted, Apollos watered, but God was causing the growth. So then neither the one who plants nor the one who waters is anything, but God who causes the growth. Now he who plants and he who waters are one; but each will receive his own reward according to his own labor. For we are God's fellow workers; you are God's field, God's building. According to the grace of God which was given to me, like a wise master builder I laid a foundation, and another is building on it. But each man must be careful how he builds on it. For no man can lay a foundation other than the one which is laid, which is Jesus Christ. (1 Cor. 3:5–11)

Men come and go; God brings them along and moves them on, for many reasons. We are called to work with a man wherever he happens to be, for as long as we have him, but always with the goal of helping him become a mature, productive disciple who can reproduce his Christian life in another.

It is a healthy practice to periodically examine what we are doing in Christian ministry. Are we bearing fruit, and if so, is it fruit that lasts? What some believe to be ministry may, in some cases, be nothing more than Christian activity, and while it may be good, it will not bear fruit that lasts.

Jesus said, "Do not work for food that spoils, but for food that endures to eternal life, which the Son of Man will give you" (John 6:27). "Do not store up for yourselves treasures on earth … but store up for yourselves treasures in heaven" (Matt. 6:19–20).

It is a wise saying that if we want to know how rich we are, we should add up everything in our lives that money cannot buy and death cannot take away. This is our heavenly treasure, including the "fruit that remains" from our lives and ministry. While much of our effort in the name of Christ may show little or no signs of lasting results, such is not the case with disciple-making. We see it in the permanently changed lives of the people to whom we have ministered and through their influence for Christ on others.

Stated yet another way, a disciple of Jesus Christ is one who learns by following another—a Christian walking in obedience to Christ who is established in the Word, prayer, witnessing, and fellowship. Are you disciple of Jesus Christ? Are you walking in obedience to His Word? Are you established in the Word, prayer, witnessing, and fellowship? If not, then strive for this goal, and then set out to reproduce your life in that of another. In other words, help someone else become an obedient believer, established in the Word, prayer, witnessing, and fellowship and capable of reproducing his or her life. This may take a long time—months or perhaps a few years— but you can make no greater investment toward the fulfillment of the Great Commission. Ask God to bring someone into your life who wants to grow spiritually, someone who is both teachable and available. Jesus has chosen us and wants to send us forth to bear lasting fruit for His kingdom. Trust Him and see what He will do through your life.

CHAPTER 6

A PRACTICAL MINISTRY

No two disciple-making situations are exactly alike with respect to the practical aspects of the ministry. Prospective disciples can be quite different from one another: age, gender, personality, temperament, education, family and socioeconomic status, church background, life experience, and more. Every convert needs acceptance, assurance, fellowship, prayer, the Word of God, and spiritual protection. As for some particular plan or routine, or the day-by-day aspects of training, what works well for one person may not work at all for another. "Whatever works best"—a way that is based on practical rather than theoretical considerations—should be our mindset when making disciples. In other words, our approach and plan must be tailored to the individual.

Practical Suggestions for the Disciple-Maker

1. Make sure that you, yourself, are living a balanced Christian life, practicing the key disciplines of Bible study, prayer, witnessing, and fellowship.
2. Be on the lookout for the hungry heart—the man who wants to grow in his relationship with Christ and is willing to meet with you.
3. Let your pastor or spiritual mentor know that you want to disciple a man. He may be an important part of the selection process by connecting you with someone. Ask God for that first man.
4. If your disciple is a recent convert, review the Gospel message with him and ask him to tell you about when he got saved. If he is

not already doing so, involve him in a church where the Bible is preached faithfully.

5.   Introduce and emphasize the importance of these fundamentals: Bible study, prayer, witnessing, and fellowship.

6.   Demonstrate to your disciple how to have a meaningful daily quiet time. Pray and study the Bible together. Share from your quiet times, as well as lessons you are learning about yourself and God. Ask him to share from his as well.

7.   Give him small bite-sized assignments in the Bible that you know will be a blessing to him.

8.   Get him in touch with others who are spending daily time with the Lord.

9.   Be available. Take time to be with him. Have him into your home. Go witnessing together. Be ready to answer truthfully whatever questions he may ask.

10.   When you are going somewhere for a day, if possible, take him with you in order to get quality, uninterrupted time together. Spend leisure time and do fun things together.

11.   Check up on your man regularly and encourage him. Assure him of you availability and willingness to help him as needed.

12.   Share and impart your vision for spiritual reproduction. When he is ready, encourage your disciple to look for a man he can disciple.

13.   Show him how to witness in his everyday experience: his family, school or workplace, neighborhood—even his church.

14.   Involve him in a small group setting for Bible study, fellowship, and prayer.

15.   Don't be afraid to challenge your disciple. God's men are resilient!

16.   Don't shoot the breeze when you get together. Don't waste time with nonessentials or less important matters. Redeem the time; stick to your specific biblical goals.

17.   Exercise patience and understanding with your man.

18.   Show him how to memorize Bible verses. Challenge him and check up on him. Make sure you are doing what you want him to do.

19.   Expose him to other teachers and leaders.

20.   Be sensitive to, and look for, teachable moments.

21.   Recognize adversity that comes into his life; these times are opportunities for spiritual growth.

22. As appropriate, incorporate into your ministry methods and elements that helped you when you were a growing disciple.
23. Maintain a support base even when he is on his own.

The Indispensable Quiet Time

The spiritual disciplines associated with the Bible are essential for a growing Christian. You should help your disciple form solid convictions about the Word of God and how he can read and study it most effectively. The following article provides a means of doing this. The suggestions that follow are taken from my pamphlet, *Helpful Hints for Reading the Bible.*

People often approach the Bible as if they were reading a history book or a novel. But the Bible is not like other books—it is not just one but sixty-six separate books. Attempting to read the Bible like you read other books can result in frustration and failure. The following ideas and suggestions are offered to help you begin and maintain a regular, meaningful time of prayer and Bible reading—a daily quiet time.

1. First, you must view the Bible as the absolute, authoritative Word of God, inspired by the Holy Spirit and relevant to every area of life. It teaches us what to believe about God and about life, death, salvation, and eternity. It reveals God's purpose for the world and for the human race. It also instructs us in how we should live, what to do when we sin, and how to maintain fellowship with God.
2. Avoid the practice of reading devotional books and other Christian writings instead of the Bible. These may be beneficial, but they should only supplement your Bible reading, not replace it.
3. Make Bible reading a priority. Set aside a certain time each day and stick with it. Resolve never to miss your Bible reading, even when you are under the weather or on the go.
4. Find a certain place where you can be alone for twenty to thirty minutes (in the morning, whenever possible) or for whatever time you have. Avoid distractions; turn off the television, mobile phone, or any other device that can interrupt your Bible reading.
5. Pray before you begin. Ask God to help you understand what you read and show you how to apply it to your life. For example, you

can pray using these words from Psalm 119:169, "Let my cry come before You, O LORD; Give me understanding according to Your word," or from Psalm 119:18, "Open my eyes, that I may behold wonderful things from Your law."

6. Read from a modern translation of the Bible. You should not have to struggle to understand the English language.

7. If you are new to the Bible, avoid starting at the beginning with the goal of reading it straight through. This approach is rarely successful. Consider starting in the Gospel of Mark or John, where you will read about the life and teachings of Jesus Christ.

8. Set realistic goals and expectations as to how much or how long you should read from the Bible each day. The main thing is not how much you read but how much you understand.

9. Avoid difficult passages or sections such as those found in some of the books of the Old Testament—if you can't understand what you are reading, or if you find it tedious or otherwise hard to read, skip ahead or go to some other part of the Bible.

10. You may want to read from two or more books of the Bible every day, perhaps from both the Old and New Testaments. Don't skip around. Keep track of what you read. For example, you can put a check or date beside a chapter when you read it or by the title of a book in the table of contents after you have read it. This will enable you to develop and maintain a consistent, comprehensive, systematic approach to the Bible.

11. Write in your Bible. Make notes in the margins; underline key words, phrases, and verses. Consider keeping a notebook or journal in which you can record notable findings along with the date and a list of chapters or passages that you have read.

12. When you read the Bible, look for and write down at least one significant word, phrase, or verse to meditate on that day.

13. Although the Bible contains figures of speech and other symbolic language, its words should otherwise be understood exactly as they appear. When an expression is out of character with the thing described, it may be considered figurative, such as in Psalm 91:4: "He will cover you with His pinions, and under His wings you may seek refuge."

14. Ask someone to encourage you and hold you accountable for reading the Bible every day. Do the same for him. Check up on each other and discuss the things you are reading.

15. There may be times when it seems like you are gaining little or nothing from your Bible reading. Read the Bible every day, even if you don't feel like it.

16. Your ability to understand the Bible will improve over time. The most important thing is that you grow in your knowledge of God and in your relationship with Jesus Christ. As the Bible says, "Grow in the grace and knowledge of our Lord and Savior Jesus Christ" (2 Peter 3:18).

17. Don't get into a rut. Periodically assess the quality of your Bible reading, making changes necessary to ensure that it continues to be a meaningful and enjoyable experience.

APPENDIX A

THE PROCESS OF DISCIPLE-MAKING

Jesus commanded His followers to "go make disciples." In light of the many references in the Gospels and Acts to those who were called disciples, we might expect disciple-making to be a major theme in the writings of Paul, Peter, John, and the others. Yet the words *disciple, disciple-making,* and *discipleship* are curiously absent from the New Testament epistles.

What is a disciple? A disciple is, foremost, a learner—one who follows the teachings of another. A disciple of Jesus Christ is one who is ever learning from Him and, through use and practice, is growing in his commitment to a Christian lifestyle.

I would like to consider disciple-making as a process—not only what one Christian can do in the life of another but what the church can do for its individual members. When Jesus issued the Great Commission, He was speaking to them collectively, as a body. The only way a body can do anything is through the cooperative participation of its individual parts (1 Cor. 12). I am not aware of any specific biblical command for one Christian, all by himself, to make a disciple, yet I believe that we should each be a part of the process.

Note some of the words that the New Testament writers use to describe the processes of disciple-making:

Parakaleo: to exhort, encourage, comfort, console (occurs 105 times)
Oikodomeo: to edify, build up (occurs thirty-seven times)
Sterizo: to establish, confirm, strengthen (occurs fourteen times)
Katecheo: to instruct (occurs seven times)
Didasko: to teach (occurs ninety-one times)
Kerusso: to proclaim (occurs sixty times)

All of these go into the making of a disciple of Jesus Christ. It can be said that a disciple is the result of all of the influences brought to bear upon a Christian's life, whether by a few or by many: preaching, teaching, instructing, establishing, confirming, strengthening, edifying, building up, exhorting, modeling, and loving.

The church needs to understand the role of personal disciple-making and one-on-one ministry in the fulfillment of the Great Commission. How much of the disciple-making process can be carried out by one person in the life of another? One might conclude that most of it can be accomplished if a strong one-on-one relationship can be established and sustained long enough. There is certainly biblical support for this concept of disciple-making. We need only to look at Jesus and His disciples. He ministered to the twelve both individually and collectively, but He gave special attention to Peter, James, and John.

While there may be no clear references in the New Testament to one-on-one disciple-making, the Paul-Timothy and Paul-Titus relationships, along with a few others, come close. Paul may have had this in mind when he wrote these words to Timothy: "The things which you have heard from me in the presence of many witnesses, entrust these to faithful men who will be able to teach others also" (2 Tim. 2:2).

Again, the church is under Christ's mandate to "go make disciples." What is your role in this process?

APPENDIX B

THE SCRIPTURES AND THE POWER OF GOD

Jesus' opponents often attempted to trap Him into saying or doing something that they could use against Him. On one occasion, when questioned by the Jewish high priests, Jesus answered and said to them, "You are mistaken, not understanding the Scriptures nor the power of God" (Matt. 22:29). The religious leaders did not know their own scriptures. They were mistaken about many things: the way of salvation, the Messiah, the future resurrection, the afterlife, heaven, the power of God, and so forth.

Jesus' statement about the scriptures and the power of God is as true today as it was then, even among Christians. How well do you know the scriptures? Have you experienced the power of God in your life? Growth and maturity in Christ cannot be measured by how long a person has been a Christian or attended church, or by how involved he has been in Christian activities. It must be measured, rather, by how well he knows the Savior and the degree to which he has applied the scriptures to his life.

The religious leaders of Jesus' day did not know the power of God, nor did they even know God. Their religion was based upon traditions, rituals, and dead works—things that can never lead to salvation. The power of God can be seen throughout the Bible. Moses, leading two million Israelites out of Egypt, called upon God to separate the waters of the Red Sea. "Stand still and see the salvation of the Lord which He will accomplish this day" (Exod. 14:13). Jesus healed a demon-possessed boy, "and they were all amazed at the mighty power of God" (Luke 9:43). The apostle Peter wrote, "Christians are kept by the power of God through faith for salvation ready to be revealed in the last time" (1 Pet. 2:5).

My brother, a twenty-year veteran of the US Navy, served aboard the aircraft carrier USS *Enterprise*, a vessel powered by eight nuclear reactors.

Later in life, he owned a small boat driven by a forty-horsepower outboard motor. Figuratively speaking, Christians too often settle for an outboard motor when they have at their disposal the powerful engines of a navy warship. According to the Gospels, on at least three occasions, Jesus said to His disciples, "O ye of little faith."

God's amazing power is available to each of us for the asking, limited only by how much faith we are willing to place in Him. Through faith, prayer, and Bible study, we can gain a more in-depth understanding of the scriptures; we can know Jesus Christ more intimately and experience the power of God in our lives as never before.

Jesus' words to the Sadducees are also relevant to a disciple-making ministry. Indeed, it is the Bible that commands, instructs, and shows us the way. Similarly, we cannot make disciples of Jesus Christ without the power and activity of the Spirit of God. Jesus said to His first disciples, "I will make you fishers of men" (Matt. 4:19). When He commanded them to go make disciples (Matt. 28:19), He sent them out in the power of the Holy Spirit. The scriptures and the power of God, therefore, are vital to success in disciple-making.

APPENDIX C

BIBLE EXERCISES FOR THE GROWING CHRISTIAN

The following exercises are designed to help a person learn his way around the Bible by locating selected verses and answering basic questions drawn from these verses. The disciple-maker should assign these exercises to his disciple, perhaps one lesson each week, and follow up by reviewing and discussing them with him.

Assurance

1. How can we know that we are children of God? (Romans 8:16)
2. How can we know that we live in Christ and that He lives in us? (1 John 4:13)
3. What three things result from hearing and believing the Gospel? (John 5:24)
4. What assurances did Jesus give to those who believe in Him? (John 10:27–29)
5. After we confess our sins to God, what else must we do? (Proverbs 28:13)
6. David makes twelve requests of God in this psalm of repentance. List six. (Psalm 51:1–2; 7–14)
7. What three things does Jesus tell us to do in prayer? (Matthew 7:7–8)
8. What promise does Jesus make in John 14:13–14?
9. As Christians, who is the source of our strength? (Philippians 4:13)
10. What is God's promise in Hebrews 13:5?
11. From where does victory, or deliverance from temptation, come? (1 Corinthians 15:57)

12. What promise can we claim from Psalm 32:8?
13. To what does the writer compare the Word of God? (Psalm 119:105) Why do you think this is a good comparison?
14. What does the Bible promise one who endures trials or temptations? (James 1:12)
15. What takes place when a person becomes a Christian? (2 Corinthians 5:17)

Your Quiet Time

1. What should we seek as we meet daily with God? (Psalm 143:8)
2. What is perhaps the best time to seek fellowship with God? (Psalm 5:3; 143:8)
3. For whom should we pray? Ephesians 6:18 _____James 5:16 _____
4. How often should we pray? What do you think this means? (1 Thessalonians 5:17)
5. In what circumstances should we give thanks? Why? (1 Thessalonians 5:18)
6. For what can we pray as we begin our quiet time? (Psalm 119:18)
7. Why must we spend regular time in the Bible and prayer? (2 Timothy 3:16–17)
8. What comes from meditating on the Word of God? (Psalm 1:2–3)
9. What word does the writer use to describe one who reads the Bible? (Revelation 1:3)
10. What does Matthew 6:6 teach about prayer?

The Word of God

1. What two things come from spending consistent time in the Word of God? (Joshua 1:8)
2. What instruction did Paul write to Timothy? (2 Timothy 2:15)
3. What great truth do these verses teach about God's Word? (Psalm 119:89; Matthew 24:35)
4. What attitude comes from hiding God's Word in our heart? (Psalm 40:8)
5. What does God command about His Word? (Deuteronomy 11:18–21)
6. What is the source of all scripture? (2 Timothy 3:16; 2 Peter 1:20–21)

7. What comes from hearing the Word of God, according to this verse? (Romans 10:17)
8. What is the Christian's responsibility regarding the Word of God? (Deuteronomy 6:17; James 1:22)
9. What do these verses teach about the Word of God? (James 1:21; 1 Peter 1:23)
10. In what way is the Word of God like a sword? (Hebrews 4:12)

The Balanced Christian Life

1. What does Jesus demand of His followers? (Mark 8:34) What do you think this means?
2. What must we, as Christians, confess about Jesus Christ? (Romans 10:9)
3. What promises does Jesus make to those who obey Him? (John 14:21)
4. How is Christ like the hub of a wheel? (John 15:5)
5. How does Paul refer to the scriptures in Acts 20:32?
6. What two things does this verse say that the Word of God can do? (Acts 20:32)
7. Why is this verse so important? (Hebrews 10:25)
8. With whom do we have fellowship? (1 John 1:3; 1 John 1:7)
9. What does it mean to witness for Christ? (1 John 1:3; Luke 8:39)
10. Why should we not worry as we witness for Christ? (Matthew 10:19–20)

Your Personal Testimony

1. What preparation does Peter instruct his readers to make? (1 Peter 3:15)
2. What was the Samaritan woman's testimony to the men of the city? (John 4:28–30)
3. What did Jesus command the healed, demon-possessed man? (Luke 8:39)
4. What did the Lord say that Paul would include in his testimony? (Acts 22:15)
5. To what does Paul give personal testimony or witness? (2 Timothy 1:12)
6. Why should we not be ashamed to tell others what Christ has done in our lives? (Romans 1:16)
7. We should not fear when we share our testimony. What three things describe God as we trust Him? (Psalm 27:1)

8. The apostles testified that they had encountered Christ in three ways. What are they? (1 John 1:1)
9. What did Job testify about Jesus Christ? (Job 19:25)
10. What promise is given in Peter's sermon? (Acts 10:43)

Sharing the Gospel

1. Who has committed sin? (Romans 3:23; Ecclesiastes 7:20)
2. What does the law (God's commandments) cause people to know? (Romans 3:20)
3. What is God's view of worldly wisdom and philosophy? (1 Corinthians 1:20)
4. How does God regard religions and traditions in connection with obtaining salvation? (Mark 7:7–8)
5. What is the result of sin? (Isaiah 59:2; Romans 6:23)
6. What happens after death? (Hebrews 9:27–28)
7. How will God treat those who refuse to believe in Jesus? (2 Thessalonians 1:8–9)
8. In what way did Mary conceive Jesus? (Matthew 1:18)
9. What is the meaning the name "Immanuel"? (Matthew 1:23)
10. Why did Jesus suffer and die? (1 Peter 3:18)
11. Where was Jesus' body laid after He died on the cross? (John 19:41–42)
12. What happened three days after Jesus was buried? (Matthew 28:6–7)
13. How can you obtain eternal life? (John 5:24)
14. According to the scriptures, what must we believe for salvation? (1 Corinthians 15:3–4)
15. What must we do to keep from perishing? (Luke 13:3)
16. What are the two basic elements of the Gospel? (Acts 20:21)
17. What happens to one who truly believes and invites Jesus into his heart? (John 1:12)
18. Who cannot go with Jesus into heaven? (John 8:24)

Spiritual Reproduction

1. What was the first thing God told Adam and Eve to do? (Genesis 1:28)
2. God created man and woman equally by separate acts of creation. In what form were they created? (Genesis 1:26–27)

3. God commanded that all living things reproduce according to their own _____. (Genesis 1:11–12, 21, 24)
4. What kind of tree will bring forth good fruit? (Matthew 7:17–18)
5. What kind of Christians will bear fruit? (John 15:4–5)
6. Describe four ways to abide in Christ:
   John 15:7 _____
   John 15:7 _____
   John 15:10 _____
   John 15:16 _____
7. How does 2 Timothy 2:2 relate to the topic of spiritual multiplication?
8. What command of Jesus can best be carried out through spiritual reproduction? (Matthew 28:19–20)
9. What was God's promise to Israel? (Deuteronomy 6:3)
10. What takes place when the Word of God is faithfully spread? (Acts 6:7)
11. How many generations did the blessing of Job's life extend to? (Job 42:16)

Helping a New Christian

Follow-up is the term often used to refer to helping a new believer get started in the Christian life. Paul may be our best biblical example in following-up new believers.

1. How did Paul refer to Christians who were not yet spiritually mature? (1 Corinthians 3:1)
2. Explain how Paul did follow-up in Acts 14:21–22 and 15:36.
3. What two family relationships does Paul use to describe his spiritual relationship with the Thessalonian Christians? (1 Thessalonians 2:7 and 2:11)
4. What was Paul's goal in following-up and discipling the Colossians? (Colossians 1:28)
5. What four things did Paul want the Philippians to imitate from his own life? (Philippians 4:9)
6. What did Paul challenge the Colossians to do? (Colossians 2:6–7)
7. Why did Paul send Timothy, his disciple, to the Thessalonians? (1 Thessalonians 3:1–2)
8. Titus, one of Paul's disciples, was dear to him. What does he call Titus in 2 Corinthians 2:13?

9. What greeting does Paul use to illustrate his devotion to the spiritual well-being of the Galatians? (Galatians 4:19)
10. What ministry was given to prophets, evangelists, and pastor-teachers? (Ephesians 4:11–12)

NOTES

Chapter 1
1   Andrew Murray, *Abide in Christ* (Urhichville, OH: Barbour and Company, 1985), 17.

Chapter 2
1   William MacDonald, *True Discipleship* (Kansas City, KS: Walterick Publishers, 1975), 5.
2   Andrew Murray, *Abide in Christ*, 5.
3   William MacDonald, *True Discipleship*, 9.

Chapter 3
1   Christopher B. Adsit, *Personal Disciple-Making* (Orlando, FL: Campus Crusade for Christ, 1996), 35.
2   Clayton Bell in the May–June 1986 issue of *Preaching* magazine.

Chapter 4
1   Oswald Chambers, *My Utmost for His Highest* (Grand Rapids, MI: Discovery House Publishers, 1992), April 24.
2   Robert Coleman, *The Master Plan of Evangelism and Discipleship* (Grand Rapids, MI: Fleming H. Revel, 1972), 45.
3   LeRoy Eims, *The Lost Art of Disciple-Making* (Grand Rapids, MI: Zondervan, 1978), 45–46.
4   Walt Henrichsen, *Disciples Are Made—Not Born* (Wheaton, IL: Victor Books, 1974), 72.
5   Scott Morton, *Down to Earth Discipling* (Colorado Springs, CO: Navpress, 2005), 55–56.

Chapter 5
1   Roy Robertson, *The Timothy Principle* (Singapore: The Navigators, Singapore, 1986), 11–12.

2   Dawson Trotman was the founder of "The Navigators."

3   Robert Coleman, *The Master Plan of Evangelism and Discipleship*, 102–103.

4   The story of this remarkable missionary can be found in his biography, *On the Golden Shore*, by Courtney Anderson (Boston, MA: Little, Brown, and Company, 1956).

5   David Livingstone was a Scottish physician, Congregationalist, and pioneer Christian missionary with the London Missionary Society, an explorer in Africa, and one of the most popular British heroes of the late-nineteenth-century Victorian era.

BOOK 2
The Biblical Meaning of Greatness

CONTENTS

"He will be great and will be called the Son of the Most High."
—Luke 1:32

INTRODUCTION

The idea for writing about biblical greatness came to me as I was pondering what the angel Gabriel said about John the Baptist: "For he will be great in the sight of the Lord" (Luke 1:15). What was it about John the Baptist that made him great in the Lord's sight? Are there others in the Bible whom the Lord calls great? If so, who are they and what made them great? Should we who are Christians seek greatness for ourselves, and if so, where do we begin? Is it possible for every Christian to attain the same kind of greatness that can be found in these biblical characters?

Napoleon Bonaparte, the military leader and two-time emperor of France, boasted, "In our time no one has a conception of what is great. It is up to me to show them." How unlike the attitude God requires: "But you, are you seeking great things for yourself? Do not seek them" (Jer. 45:5).

In the 1960s, a famous athlete dazzled the sports world with this boisterous claim: "I am the greatest! I am the greatest! I am the greatest." Indeed he was the greatest for a while, but then someone else came along, and someone after that, whose performance in that sport earned them the title. Every area of human endeavor has its great men and women: athletics, entertainment, politics, science, pioneering, inventing, arts, military. Those who reach the pinnacle of their field are usually labeled "great." Would anyone deny such a title to Beethoven, Lincoln, Edison, or Einstein?

Greatness by human standards sets some people apart from others, and human society is quick to recognize, applaud, and even idolize those who possess it. Athletes, entertainers, and Hollywood celebrities become heroes, icons, and role models (though not always good ones). Human greatness seems to have a powerful effect upon people, and most of us are naturally drawn to those who possess it. Thus well-known and famous people are often called upon to promote noteworthy causes or crusades. Yet this greatness offers nothing of lasting or eternal value.

Jesus said, "For what does it profit a man to gain the whole world, and forfeit his soul? For what will a man give in exchange for his soul?" (Mark 8:36–37). On the other hand, those who choose to focus on things of eternal value and significance soon come to understand the shallow and fleeting nature of what the world considers great. As a matter of fact, after those deemed great by the world have been exalted and praised for a season, they are often forgotten altogether.

In Jesus' day, as in ours, people held erroneous views of greatness. To the religious leaders of Israel, greatness was keeping the Law of Moses, gaining recognition in the marketplaces, and exercising power and authority over the people. Yet what they possessed was not greatness at all but rather pride and hypocrisy, as noted in this Pharisee's prayer: "The Pharisee stood and was praying this to himself: 'God, I thank You that I am not like other people: swindlers, unjust, adulterers, or even like this tax collector: I fast twice a week; I pay tithes of all that I get'" (Luke 18:11–12).

The Bible records the story of a "man named Simon, who formerly was practicing magic in the city and astonishing the people of Samaria, claiming to be someone great; and they all, from smallest to greatest, were giving attention to him, saying, 'This man is what is called the Great Power of God'"(Acts 8:10). This was an individual who practiced magic, proclaimed himself great, and soon had others calling him great as well. How willing people are to accept what is nothing more than a façade of greatness when it is foisted upon them.

There is nothing wrong with attributing greatness to people, places, ideas, or events, provided the word *great* is properly applied. It is, rather, its misapplication that should concern us. What is the standard against which genuine greatness should be measured? Who or what determines whether someone or something can be considered great? In what sense, if any, should a Christian pursue this virtue? These are some of the questions that will be discussed in this book.

The title and scope of this book demand that we begin with how the words *great* and *greatness* are used in the Bible. As for biblical greatness, Jesus defines it, embodies it, and models it. It is an expression of true discipleship.

CHAPTER 1

THE CHARACTER OF GOD

Greatness Ascribed

"Great is the LORD and highly to be praised, and His greatness is unsearchable."

—Psalm 145:3

The word *greatness* is found thirty-two times in the Bible. It is ascribed first and foremost to God Himself—to His name, His attributes, and His works.

- "For I proclaim the name of the LORD; ascribe greatness to our God!" (Deut. 32:3).
- "Yours, O LORD, is the greatness and the power and the glory and the victory and the majesty; indeed everything that is in the heavens and the earth; Yours is the dominion, O LORD, and You do exalt Yourself as head over all" (1 Chron. 29:11).
- "Praise Him for His mighty deeds; praise Him according to His excellent greatness" (Ps. 150:2).
- "They were all amazed at the greatness of God" (Luke 9:43).
- "The surpassing greatness of His power toward us who believe" (Eph. 1:19).

Every aspect of God's nature can be labeled *great*—God's great love, mercy, compassion, kindness, and so forth. These attributes are great because He is great; they are manifestations of His divine essence. For the same reason, His works and wonders are great, as declared repeatedly in Psalms. The Bible says, "In the beginning God created the heavens and the earth" (Gen. 1:1). Could there be a more commanding testimony of the greatness of God than what we see in the world around us?

Even a young child recognizes the greatness of God, praying, "God is great, and God is good; let us thank Him for our food. By His hands we all are fed; thank You for our daily bread. Amen."

The songwriter expresses it beautifully in the hymn "How Great Thou Art":

> Oh Lord, my God, when I in awesome wonder
> Consider all the worlds Thy hands have made.
> I see the stars; I hear the rolling thunder
> Thy power throughout the universe displayed.
> Then sings my soul, my Savior God to Thee
> How great Thou art, how great Thou art.
> Then sings my soul, my Savior God to Thee
> How great Thou art, how great Thou art.

Greatness is also ascribed to Jesus Christ:

- "He will be great and will be called the Son of the Most High; and the Lord God will give him the throne of his father David" (Luke 1:32).
- "Fear gripped them all, and they began glorifying God, saying, 'A great prophet has arisen among us!' and, 'God has visited His people'" (Luke 7:16).
- "Looking for the blessed hope and the appearing of the glory of our great God and Savior, Christ Jesus" (Titus 2:13).
- "Therefore, since we have a great high priest who has passed through the heavens, Jesus the Son of God, let us hold fast our confession" (Heb. 4:14).
- "Now the God of peace, who brought up from the dead the great Shepherd of the sheep through the blood of the eternal covenant, even Jesus our Lord" (Heb. 13:20).

The Bible declares Jesus Christ to be God Himself in human flesh. Therefore, any particular quality ascribed to God can and must be equally ascribed to Jesus Christ—and vice versa. The names of God are often applied to Jesus. He is called "the Mighty God, the Everlasting Father," and "Immanuel" (meaning "God with us"). Elsewhere, Jesus is called "The Lord (Jehovah) our Righteousness," "God," and "Son of God." The Bible ascribes the characteristics of deity to Jesus Christ. He is described as eternal, omnipresent, omniscient, omnipotent, and immutable. Jesus Christ is equal with God the Father. He is worshiped as God. His name is assigned equal standing with God the Father in the church's baptismal formula and in the Apostolic Benediction.[1] Christ performed works that only God can do. He is the Creator. He is the upholder of all things. He forgives sin. He will raise the dead and execute judgment.

God is not great because of what He has done, what He is now doing, or what He will do. These things are evidence of His greatness—not the cause or reason for it. (Note the same logic as in this simple theological premise: "We are not sinners because we sin; we sin because we are sinners.") God's greatness must have inspired the psalmist to write, "One generation shall praise your works to another, and shall declare your mighty acts. On the glorious splendor of Your majesty, and on Your wonderful works, I will meditate. Men shall speak of the power of your awesome acts, and I will tell of Your greatness" (Ps. 145:4–6).

The greatness of God is found experientially only by those who respond to God's invitation, those who draw near to Him. When they do, they discover that He is a God of order and redemptive love. Hebrews 11:6 says, "And without faith it is impossible to please him, for he who comes to God must believe that he exists and that he is a rewarder of those who earnestly seek him." Do not say that you cannot reach God. In faith, draw near to Him, and He will draw near to you. That is always the offer of scripture.

Apart from being attributed to God, the word *great* is ascribed directly to only a few people in the Bible. For example, God said to Abraham, "I will bless you, and make your name great" (Gen. 12:2).

The author of the epistle to the Hebrews wrote about Melchizedek, "Now observe how great this man was to whom Abraham, the patriarch, gave a tenth of the choicest spoils … but without any dispute the lesser is blessed by the greater" (Heb. 7:4,7).

Esther records the following about Mordecai, the Jew:

> And all the accomplishments of his authority and strength, and the full account of the greatness of Mordecai to which the king advanced him, are they not written in the Book of the Chronicles of the Kings of Media and Persia? For

Mordecai the Jew was second only to King Ahasuerus, and great among the Jews and in favor with his many kinsmen, one who sought the good of his people and one who spoke for the welfare of his whole nation. (Esther 10:2–3)

Second Kings 5:1 says, "Now Naaman, captain of the army of the king of Aram, was a great man with his master, and highly respected, because by him the LORD had given victory to Aram." Similarly, the Bible attributes greatness to Jacob, Joseph, Ephraim, Moses, David, Solomon, Jonah, and Job. Furthermore, if greatness is based upon the possession of the same qualities, attributes, or accomplishments seen in these men, then could not others who possess these same qualities be called great? There are many such people in the Bible: Joshua, Samuel, Elijah, Elisha, Hezekiah, Esther, Ruth, Peter, and Paul. Greatness is also ascribed to Israel and the people of God: "And I will make you a great nation, and I will bless you, and make your name great; and so you shall be a blessing" (Gen. 12:2).

Ray Stedman provides a fitting application and closing to this discussion of the greatness of God:

Our Father, how pitifully weak are words to express the greatness of your deeds and actions among men! How little have we understood the wonders of life that surround us on every side! How blind we have been to the simplest things of our nature and of our lives! Lord, we pray that you will open our eyes to see something more of your greatness and the fact that you have been moving in history and in our own lives. Millions today can testify to your greatness, to your redeeming love, and to your supernatural activity, doing things that no man can do. When we see a man or a woman changed, released from habits of thought, and made over into a new creature, what greater testimony is needed that here is a supernatural thing! Man cannot do it. All our struggling, all our educative processes, all our attempts by legislation to change men have been of no avail. But this simple blessed word of the gospel, how it changes human hearts and sets men free.[2]

C H A P T E R   2

NO ORDINARY MAN

Greatness Bestowed

"He will be great in the sight of the Lord."

—Luke 1:15

A gifted high school musician was often commended by his instructor for his exceptional performance on the violin. When the young man performed at a renowned music festival, a world-famous violinist happened to hear him play and went on to praise him publicly for such a fine display of musicianship. Never before had the young man felt so good about his playing. The praise of such a virtuoso was priceless. It seems that praise can be measured by the worth of the one issuing it. If this is true, then no man ever received such praise as John the Baptist. Jesus called him "a shining light" and "more than a prophet." "Truly I say to you, among those born of women there has not arisen anyone greater than John the Baptist" (Matt. 11:11).

John the Baptist was ordained by God to announce the long-awaited coming of the Messiah, as foretold by the prophets Isaiah and Malachi. Although he was in line to become a priest, John would instead be a prophet. His name means "The Lord has been gracious." By his birth, God was indeed gracious to John's aging parents, Zacharias and Elizabeth. The angel Gabriel had spoken to Zacharias the priest about his son-to-be. Soon afterward, Mary went to visit Elizabeth. "When Elizabeth heard Mary's greeting, the baby leaped in her womb and Elizabeth was filled with the Holy Spirit" (Luke 1:41).

How did John, still in his mother's womb, recognize Jesus? As prophesied by the angel of the Lord, John was also filled with the Holy Spirit even before he was born (Luke 1:15). And the Holy Spirit in John bore witness to the fact that the Messiah was nearby. How fitting that the forerunner and herald of the coming King would be the first to recognize Him.

From birth, John was set apart as a Nazirite. During the term of his consecration, a Nazirite was bound to abstain from wine, grapes, every product of the vine, and from every kind of intoxicating drink. He was forbidden to cut his hair or to approach any dead body, even that of his nearest relative.

He would sometimes separate himself from other people in order to eliminate distractions. Most Nazirites took a vow for a set period of time— usually from thirty to one hundred days. (Samson and Samuel were also dedicated as Nazirites from birth.)

All that is known of the period between John's birth and the beginning of his public ministry is found in a single verse: "And the child continued to grow and to become strong in spirit, and he lived in the deserts until the day of his public appearance to Israel" (Luke 1:80). Solitary communion with God prepared him for his work. He went forth, his very appearance indicative of the separation from the world in which he preached. His clothing was made of camel's hair bound with a leather girdle; his food, that which was supplied by the desert—locusts and wild honey.

Greatness was bestowed upon John, yet it would come only through the prophet's total devotion to God. John resembled Elijah the prophet, whom God had sent nine hundred years earlier to call Israel to repentance and to warn it of the judgment to come. Just as Elijah's preaching had drawn people to God, John's would turn many from their unbelief to repentance. His message broke four hundred years of silence and gave new hope to the nation. Like Elijah, John isolated himself from society and was ready to rebuke both kings and multitudes. This included Herod and his illegitimate wife, Herodias—reminiscent of the actions of Elijah in rebuking Ahab, the king of Israel, and his wicked wife, Jezebel (1 Kings 21). The lives of both prophets protested the corrupt societies of their day. Each man came onto the scene suddenly and with vigor. John's message was one of repentance for entrance into Christ's Messianic kingdom—even for the self-righteous religious leaders of Israel. His asceticism[1] was a genuine expression of his character and the means by which he would reach the masses. John's abstinence from the world was so great that some thought him possessed: "He has a demon" (Luke 7:33)!

The memory of his zeal and the lasting effect of his work continued both in his disciples and in the early church. In Acts 18:24–28, we read about those, like Apollos, who did not know who Jesus was but who spread the Gospel based on what John the Baptist taught them. We read in Acts 19:1–6 that the apostle Paul, while in Ephesus, encountered some believers who were taught and baptized by John but who knew nothing about being converted and receiving God's Spirit. He was truly the greatest among all the Old Testament prophets.

God had empowered John with the Holy Spirit, hence the people's great response to his preaching. "For he will be great in the sight of the Lord; and he will drink no wine or liquor, and he will be filled with the Holy Spirit while yet in his mother's womb. And he will turn many of the sons of Israel back to the Lord their God" (Luke 1:15).

Always under the Spirit's control, John sought nothing for himself. He was a humble servant of God who had a tremendous impact on those in Jerusalem and Judea, even after his death, for His name had become well known. People were saying, "John the Baptist has risen from the dead, and that is why these miraculous powers are at work in Him" (Mark 6:14). The memory of his zeal and the lasting effect of his work continued in both his disciples and in the early church.

Though John was full of boldness and fire, his life, as noted above, was characterized by humility and self-denial. He declined the honors that an admiring public almost forced upon him. Instead, he declared himself to be insignificant, merely a voice calling upon the people to prepare to receive the one whose sandals he was "not fit to remove" (Matt. 3:11). When Christ came, John enjoined his own disciples to attach themselves to Him, gracefully acknowledging the fact that Jesus must be given the preeminence and that he, himself, must decrease. For his courage in speaking the truth to King Herod, he went to prison and eventually to death. From the world's perspective, John was neither great nor important, yet in the sight of the Lord, he was both. His humility and servanthood are unmistakable signs of true greatness.

When we come to realize that God has given us a specific purpose for our lives, we can move forward with confidence, fully trusting the one who called us. Like John the Baptist, we can live without fear, focusing on our

God-given mission. Can there be any greater joy or fulfillment in this life than knowing that God's pleasure and reward await us in heaven?

What role do such things play in your life? Can people view you as abstaining from the world, even to the point of misunderstanding who you are or what you stand for? In our attitude toward the world, we should follow the example of John the Baptist, while heeding the words of the apostle John:

> Do not love the world or the things in the world. If anyone loves the world, the love of the Father is not in him. For all that is in the world, the lust of the flesh and the lust of the eyes and the boastful pride of life, is not from the Father, but is from the world. The world is passing away, and also its lusts; but the one who does the will of God lives forever. (1 John 2:15–17)

Jesus Christ must be given first place in our lives. If our hearts are truly set upon serving and obeying Him, we should have little difficulty assigning the proper value to worldly attractions. Since John the Baptist was great in the sight of the Lord, and since he had renounced everything that the world esteems of any value (worldly possessions, fame, authority, power), personal greatness in God's sight must be unrelated to individual accomplishments or family heritage.

CHAPTER 3

CALLED BY GOD

Greatness Attained

"Now the man Moses was very humble, more than any
man who was on the face of the earth."

—Numbers 12:3

One of my earliest childhood memories of church is that of the colorful
pictures of Bible stories given to us each week in Sunday school. I
particularly remember the one showing the baby Moses being discovered
by Pharaoh's daughter as he floated in a reed basket along the banks of the
Nile River. An expression of curiosity and delight can be seen on the faces
of the princess and her attendants, while a young girl—Miriam, Moses'
sister—hides nearby, looking on from among the reeds. These bright,
colorful pictures were an appropriate introduction to some of the most
important characters in the Bible. I am thankful for this early memory—a
reminder of the humble origin of one who would achieve greatness in the
sight of God.

Although Moses lived fifteen hundred years before Jesus, he came
to possess the same attributes that Jesus used to define greatness. The
Hebrews had been in bondage to Egypt for more than four hundred
years. The king of Egypt, fearful that the increasing Hebrew population
would pose a threat to the Egyptians, gave an order to kill every newborn
boy: "Every son who is born you are to cast into the Nile" (Exod. 1:22).
To protect Moses, his mother set him afloat in the Nile, trusting God to
protect him.

Reared as a son in Pharaoh's house, Moses became great by the world's standards, yet he would forfeit everything on his journey toward true greatness. Bible scholars agree that if any person in the Old Testament could be called great, it would be Moses:

> Since that time no prophet has risen in Israel like Moses, whom the LORD knew face to face, for all the signs and wonders which the LORD sent him to perform in the land of Egypt against Pharaoh, all his servants, and all his land, and for all the mighty power and for all the great terror which Moses performed in the sight of all Israel. (Deut. 34:10–12)

Is there something in the path of your spiritual progress that you must relinquish before you can begin or resume your own journey toward biblical greatness? Could there be some sin, some unhealthy practice, or unwholesome relationship? Is your life unduly focused upon money, material possessions, or worldly ambitions? Anything that is not pleasing to God can hinder your pursuit of greatness.

After killing an Egyptian in defense of a Hebrew, Moses was forced to flee Egypt and the life he had known in Pharaoh's house. For forty years, he lived in the desert as a shepherd until he was called by God and commissioned for a special assignment (Exod. 3–4). Speaking from a burning bush, God charged Moses with the task of leading the Hebrews from Egypt to the Promised Land, the land of Canaan. This calling also involved receiving the written Law on Mount Sinai, governing the new nation in the wilderness, and overseeing the building of the Tabernacle. It also included establishing the institution of the formal worship of God through the Levitical priesthood.[1]

Moses' sense of inadequacy can be seen by the volley of excuses that he returned when God, speaking from the bush, told him to go to Egypt: "What if they do not believe me or listen to me?" "Who am I, that I should do this?" "Who shall I say sent me?" "I am not eloquent." "Let someone else do it." But God had called Moses to this mission, and He would give him the strength, guidance, and ability to complete it.

What excuses have you offered God for not doing something He wants you to do? Are you afraid or unwilling to trust Him? Is the memory of some past failure, like that of Moses, hindering you? The call of God does not depend upon our own gifts or abilities, our past performance, or our self-image. When He calls, we must obey. God will give us the ability to carry out His will.

Roger Staubach, who led the Dallas Cowboys to the world championship in 1971, admitted that his position as a quarterback who didn't call his own signals was a source of trial for him. Coach Landry sent in every play. He told Roger when to pass and when to run, and only in emergency situations could he change the play (and he had better be right!). Even though Roger considered Coach Landry to have a "genius mind" when it came to football strategy, pride said that he should be able to run his own team. Roger later said, "I faced up to the issue of obedience. Once I learned to obey, there was harmony, fulfillment, and victory"(source unknown).

God sent a series of plagues upon the land of Egypt, causing Pharaoh to release the Hebrews. Soon after leaving Egypt, the people began to complain about the difficulties of life in the desert. Because of their rebellion (a clear indication of their failure to trust God), they spent the next forty years on a journey that should have taken ten days. Over and over again, they angered God, but Moses continued to intervene with God on their behalf. One of the marks of greatness seen in Moses was his humility before God. "Now the man Moses was very humble, more than any man who was on the face of the earth" (Num. 12:3).

Moses exemplified not only humility but that other attribute of true greatness—the spirit of a servant. God called him "Moses My servant" (Josh. 1:2). Moses undertook nothing without God's guidance. His former attitude of self-confidence and impetuosity gave place to meekness, patience, and long-suffering. He was to experience perseverance under relentless provocation and trials from an obstinate people. Until the day he died, Moses remained a humble servant of God and of the people whom God entrusted to his care.

Yet he, himself, never entered the Promised Land. On one occasion, he failed to trust and honor God as holy before the people (Num. 20). When told by God to speak to a rock in order to obtain water, in an unsympathetic spirit that God calls rebellion, Moses struck the rock instead. Because of this single act of disobedience, God forbade him from crossing the Jordan River into Canaan. Nevertheless, his humility can be seen right to at the end. He meekly submitted to God's judgment, thinking not of himself but only of God's glory and the future good of the Hebrew nation. Moses said, "May the LORD, the God of the spirits of all flesh, appoint a man over the congregation, who will go out and come in before them, and who will lead them out and bring them in" (Num. 27:16–17). The writer of Hebrews speaks in glowing terms of the faith of Moses:

> By faith Moses, when he had grown up, refused to be called the son of Pharaoh's daughter, choosing rather to endure ill-treatment with the people of God than to enjoy the passing pleasures of sin, considering the reproach of Christ greater riches than the treasures of Egypt; for he was looking to the reward. (Heb. 11:24–26)

These and other passages of scripture reveal just how highly Moses was esteemed by various biblical writers under the inspiration of the Holy Spirit. The New Testament, however, shows us that Moses' teaching was intended only to prepare humanity for the greater teaching and work of Jesus Christ. What Moses promised, Jesus fulfilled: "For the Law was given through Moses; grace and truth were realized through Jesus Christ" (John 1:17).

One can hardly study the biblical accounts of Moses without recognizing the strong typology connecting him with Christ. In the New Testament, the Greek word *týpos*, meaning "example," describes a model or pattern in the Old Testament that is fulfilled in the life and ministry of Christ. The primary person, story, or event is the type, whereas the fulfillment is the antitype. The New is in the Old concealed; the Old is in the New revealed. The apostle Paul explained it this way: "Now these things happened to them as an example, and they were written for our instruction, upon whom the ends of the ages have come" (1 Cor. 10:11). In other words, Moses is the type, a representation of Christ in the Old Testament.

CHAPTER 4

GREATNESS MISUNDERSTOOD
As the World Thinks

"But they kept silent, for on the way they had discussed
with one another which of them was the greatest."
—Mark 9:34

Years ago, Dr. H. A. Ironside, who was pastor of the prestigious Moody Church in downtown Chicago, felt that he was not as humble as he should have been. So he asked an older friend what he could do about it. The friend suggested, "Make a sandwich board with the plan of salvation in scripture on it. Put it on and walk through the business district of Chicago for a whole day." Ironside followed his friend's humiliating advice. After he got home, as he took off the sandwich board, he caught himself thinking, *There's not another person in Chicago that would be willing to do a thing like that* (unknown source).

Spiritual pride is an insidious enemy that we all continually face. It was one of the main sins of the Pharisees. They thought that they were a notch above their fellow Jews (John 9:28–34) and far above the despised Gentile dogs. To confront such pride, Jesus told the parable of the Pharisee and the publican who went up to the temple to pray (Luke 18:9–14). The Pharisee thanked God that he wasn't like the publican. But how many times have we read this story and thought, *Thank God that I'm not like that Pharisee?*

The apostle Paul apparently knew from some of his contacts in Rome that there was a problem with creeping spiritual pride on the part of the Gentile Christians against their fellow Jewish believers and unbelieving

Jews. Left unchecked, this attitude would lead to division in the church, to anti-Semitism that would choke out their witness to the Jews, and to the spiritual ruin of those who continued down that path. Mark writes, "They came to Capernaum; and when He was in the house, He began to question them, 'What were you discussing on the way?' But they kept silent, for on the way they had discussed with one another which of them was the greatest" (Mark 9:33–34).

What caused this mixed band of young men to aspire to greatness? The priests referred to them as "uneducated and untrained men ... recognizing them as having been with Jesus" (Acts 4:13). By the world's standards, it is unlikely that these would ever have been regarded as great men. It is possible that even people who choose to follow Jesus can aspire to the wrong kind of greatness. For this reason, both vocational and lay ministers sometimes find themselves of little value in the ministry. They may mistakenly believe that their association with Jesus will assure them some degree of greatness, but like His disciples, they do not understand its real meaning. Some may fall in love with the ministry itself, while missing the true mark of a disciple—humility and wholehearted devotion to Christ.

On the occasion of their dispute about greatness, the disciples had been with Jesus most of three years. They had witnessed every phase of His ministry: preaching, teaching, healing, casting out demons, performing nature miracles,[1] confounding the religious leaders—all the while gaining favor with the common people. These twelve men probably considered themselves to be the in crowd, enjoying privileges that others did not have. Even in the notoriety that was to develop later in Jesus' ministry, they must have sensed something special about who they were.

The apostle Paul writes, "For through the grace given to me I say to everyone among you not to think more highly of himself than he ought to think; but to think so as to have sound judgment, as God has allotted to each a measure of faith" (Rom. 12:3). We must be careful not to think more highly of ourselves than we should, for it is only by God working through us that we can accomplish anything of eternal significance.

Jesus sent out His disciples with power and authority to preach and to heal the sick. On one occasion, seventy-two returned joyfully from such a mission, saying, "Lord, even the demons are subject to us in your name" (Luke 10:17). Ordinary men were preaching, healing, and casting out demons. Two of them were even ready to call down fire, comparing themselves with Elijah on Mt. Carmel (1 Kings 18). Had witnessing the great works of Jesus caused the disciples to seek greatness for themselves? Had they completely misunderstood His teaching about the kingdom of heaven?

Are we sometimes too willing to accept the applause of other people for something we have accomplished only in the Lord's strength? Can we say, like Paul to the churches in Galatia, "For am I now seeking the favor of men, or of God? Or am I striving to please men? If I were still trying to please men, I would not be a bond-servant of Christ" (Gal. 1:10)?

On the day before the Passover, the disciples had located the upper room and made preparations according to Jesus' instructions. At the appointed hour, as they reclined at the table, Jesus said, "For I say to you, I shall never again eat it until it is fulfilled in the kingdom of God" (Luke 22:16); but on this same occasion, "there arose also a dispute among them as to which one of them was regarded to be greatest" (Luke 22:24).

Jesus had often spoken about the suffering that He was to endure, but His disciples failed to grasp its reality. One would think that on such a solemn occasion as the Passover meal, especially in light of what Jesus had said about His imminent suffering, these disciples would not be thinking about their own greatness. Do your own interests often draw you away from the message of the preacher or the words of your teacher? Do you sometimes focus upon your own hopes, dreams, and aspirations while instead you should be striving to find out what God would have you to do, especially regarding the needs of others? This was the case with at least two of Jesus's disciples:

> James and John, the two sons of Zebedee, came up to Jesus, saying, "Teacher, we want You to do for us whatever we ask of You." And He said to them, "What do you want Me to do for you?" They said to Him, "Grant that we may sit, one on Your right and one on Your left, in Your glory." (Mark 10:35–37)

When Jesus taught about the kingdom of heaven, He was referring to the kingdom promised to Israel by the Old Testament prophets, a kingdom over which He Himself would reign. The Jews were expecting that kingdom to be ushered in by a conquering Messiah who would set Israel free from her Roman oppressors. Blinded as to the true nature of the Messiah, who was to come first as a humble servant of God, the Jews refused to believe in Jesus and so rejected Him. The Messianic kingdom would not (and will not) be established until He comes again in power and glory.

At the sight of Elijah and Moses, when Peter, James, and John were with Jesus on the mountain, "Peter said to Jesus, 'Master, it is good for us to be here; let us make three tabernacles: one for you and one for Moses and one for Elijah'—not realizing what he was saying" (Luke 9:33). Peter wanted to celebrate the Feast of Tabernacles (Lev. 23:42), having recognized the millennial glory of Christ, but He did not understand that its fulfillment could not be realized until Jesus was publicly recognized. In any case, the disciples had heard Him teach about the coming kingdom, and they wanted their part in it. Thus they argued as to who would occupy the seats of honor next to Jesus.

Did Peter understand greatness when, at the time of Jesus' arrest, he drew a sword and cut off the ear of a servant named Malchus? Did he and two other disciples understand it when they wanted to build three tabernacles and remain with Jesus on the Mount of Transfiguration? Or when they rebuked the little children that were being brought to Jesus to bless them? The sons of Zebedee misunderstood it when they wanted to call down fire on some Samaritans who refused to receive Jesus in their village. So it went, for three years—the disciples daily in His presence yet missing the true purpose of this humble servant of God. In the months and years ahead, these same men would come to understand the true meaning of greatness as they carried the Gospel into the world and gave their lives in the work of Christ's kingdom.

CHAPTER 5

GREATNESS DEFINED

In the Words of Jesus

"The greatest among you will be your servant."
—Matthew 23:11

I was once involved in a ministry on a military base where each of us went door-to-door through the bachelor officers' quarters. Our objective was to recruit men to a weekly Bible study. After introducing ourselves, we would extend the following invitation: "Would you be interested in attending a Bible study centered upon 'what Jesus said about becoming a Christian'—if you had the time?" (This last phrase was inserted to head off the common excuse of not having enough time.) Most of the men with whom we spoke seemed to show at least a nominal interest in the subject. Some were available and willing to participate, so we launched the study as planned. Had we stated the invitation differently, such as, "Would you be interested in what the Bible says about becoming a Christian?"those men may have shown less interest. The phrase "what Jesus said" made the difference. People really do want to know what Jesus said. When He spoke, people listened.

In the Sermon on the Mount (Matt. 5–7), Jesus spoke about what it takes to be called "great" in His kingdom. "Anyone who breaks one of the least of these commandments and teaches others to do the same will be called least in the kingdom of heaven, but whoever practices and teaches these commands will be called great in the kingdom of heaven"(Matt. 5:19). It seems that the title "great" belongs only to those who obey Jesus' commands. It should be noted that there are only a few passages in the Gospels in which Jesus uses the term *great, greater,* or *greatest* with reference to the aspirations of men. As we examine these passages, what emerges is a distinct, twofold requirement for greatness—humility and servanthood—attributes that we have already seen in both John the Baptist and in Moses.

Two of Jesus' disciples, James and John, sought greatness. More than that, they craved fame and status. This is evident by a bold question proposed to Jesus: "Teacher," they said to him. "We want for you to do whatever we ask from you. Grant us to sit, one at your right hand and one at your left, in your glory" (Mark 10:35–37).

The arrogant desires of their hearts are obvious. They could have asked Jesus for anything. They didn't ask for more joy or more favor or faith or holiness or whatever. No, James and John wanted something else; they wanted glory. It's easy to beat up on the disciples. But picture yourself in the story. Do you struggle with selfish ambition? Are you sometimes motivated by selfish reasons? Do you compare yourself with others and sometimes desire good things for the wrong reasons? Thankfully, Jesus was patient with the brothers, and He is patient with us. It's interesting to note that Jesus did not rebuke them regarding their *desire* for greatness but instead gave them a new definition of greatness: "Whoever wants to become great among you must be your servant" (Mark 10:43).

So what is true greatness? The following is C.J. Mahaney's definition:

> As sinfully and culturally defined, pursuing greatness looks like this: Individuals motivated by self-interest, self-indulgence, and a false sense of self-sufficiency to pursue selfish ambition for the purpose of self-glorification. Contrast that with the pursuit of *true greatness* as biblically defined: *Serving others for the glory of God.* This is the genuine expression of humility; this is true greatness as the Savior defined it. So it's not the desire that's bad, per se, but the definition. And Jesus completely redefines what greatness is, which is serving others to the glory of God. So what is greatness? Do you now know the greatness meaning? Do you now know how to define greatness? In a word, true greatness is about *humility.*[1]

Humility

The Gospels record at least two occasions when Jesus used little children while teaching important truths about the kingdom of heaven. The first deals with humility; the second with simplicity, innocence, and childlike faith:

> At that time the disciples came to Jesus, saying, "Who then is greatest in the kingdom of heaven?" He called a little child and had him stand among them.
>
> And he said: "I tell you the truth, unless you change and become like little children, you will never enter the kingdom of heaven. Therefore, whoever humbles himself like this child is the greatest in the kingdom of heaven." (Matt. 18:2–4)

Little children are innocent, unassuming, submissive, dependent, and trusting. And just as they are a source of joy to their parents, we should be a joy to our heavenly Father. Our lives should likewise be marked by innocence, submission, dependence, and trust. These characteristics of a little child reveal something about humility, which in turn tells us about greatness.

What then is the meaning of humility? From a biblical perspective, it is not a belittling of oneself but an exalting or praising of others, especially God and Jesus. Biblical humility is also recognizing that by ourselves we are inadequate, without dignity, and worthless. Since God is both our Creator and Redeemer, our very existence and our righteousness depend on Him. Yet, because we are created in God's image and because believers are "in Christ" (Eph. 1:3–4), we have infinite worth and dignity. True humility does not produce pride but gratitude. The humble mind is at the root of all other graces and virtues. Self-exaltation spoils everything. Perhaps most importantly, there can be no real love without humility. "Love," said Paul, "does not boast, it is not proud … it is not self-seeking" (1 Cor. 13:4–5).

Dwight Hill offers the following comment in his book *Facts of the Matter*:

> Blessed are the poor in spirit, for theirs is the kingdom of heaven" (Matt. 5:3). By 'poor in spirit' He means the

spiritually destitute—those who acknowledge their utter helplessness, spiritual poverty, and lack of superiority before others; people who are painfully aware of their deadness before God. The 'poor in spirit' recognize that they are no better, no richer, no more superior to the next person, regardless of what they have achieved in this world in terms of fame, fortune, or power.[2]

In the following graphic description of what it means to be humble, Brennan Manning describes the "poor in spirit":

"Ragmuffin" believers—the unsung assembly of saved sinners who are little in their own sight, conscious of their brokenness and powerlessness before God, and who cast themselves on his mercy. Startled by the extravagant love of God, they do not require success, fame, wealth, or power to validate their worth. Their spirit transcends all distinctions between the powerful and powerless, educated and illiterate, billionaires and bag ladies, high-tech geeks and low-tech nerds, males and females, the circus and the sanctuary.[3]

When asked to explain the secret of a lifetime of successful Christian ministry, an elderly preacher responded, "I have always sought obscurity and given the glory to God!" He was echoing the psalmist who wrote, "Not to us, O LORD, not to us, but to your name be the glory, because of your love and faithfulness" (Psalm 115:1).

This is humility; but humility does not mean passive acceptance of injustice, personal affront, or letting someone walk all over you. Jesus would not have appeared humble when He made a whip and cleansed the Temple of those who were buying and selling animals for sacrifice. Neither would John the Baptist have been seen as humble when he addressed the Sadducees and Pharisees as "a brood of vipers" and provoked them with his message of repentance. Humility does not preclude expressing righteous anger or taking a stand for the truth and commands of God.

Just as the world has as unbiblical view of greatness, it also has a distorted view of humility. Andrew Murray bemoans the missing emphasis upon humility in the life of an aspiring disciple:

When I look back upon my own religious experience, or around upon the Church of Christ in the world, I stand amazed at the thought of how little humility is sought after as the distinguishing feature of the discipleship of Jesus. In preaching and living, in the daily intercourse of the home and social life, in the more special fellowship, in the direction and performance of work for Christ—how much proof there is that humility is not esteemed the cardinal virtue, the only root from which the graces can grow, the one indispensable condition of true fellowship with Jesus.[4]

Servanthood

The mother of James and John asked Jesus to grant to her sons the places of honor in His kingdom. He replied, "Whoever wants to become great among you must be your servant, and whoever wants to be first must be your slave, just as the Son of Man did not come to be served, but to serve, and to give his life as a ransom for many" (Matt. 20:26–28). Here Jesus introduces the second qualification for greatness—servanthood.

The love of God that we possess in Jesus should cause us to seek the well-being of others and to serve them. Paul wrote, "Do nothing out of selfish ambition or vain conceit, but in humility consider others better than yourselves. Each of you should look not only to your own interests, but also to the interests of others" (Phil. 2:3–4).

Some people are natural servants; others possess the spiritual gift of serving. Yet in another sense, all believers are called to serve both God and people. Jesus "went around doing good" (Acts 10:38). This is serving; we must do the same. "Therefore, as we have opportunity, let us do good to all people, especially to those who belong to the family of believers" (Gal. 6:10).

In their epistles, Paul, James, Peter, and Jude all refer to themselves as "bondservants of Jesus." How do we serve? We do so first by acknowledging Him as Lord, striving to obey Him fully, and seeking His will in every area of our lives. Jesus said, "If you love me, you will obey what I command" (John 14:15). Serving God also means serving people, yet can we truly serve people without loving them?

Paul wrote, "God, whom I serve with my whole heart in preaching the gospel of His Son" (Rom. 1:9). "The entire law is summed up in a single command: 'Love your neighbor as yourself'" (Gal. 5:14). "Though I am free and belong to no man, I make myself a slave to everyone, to win as many as possible" (1 Cor. 9:19).

How then do we serve people in a way that meets Jesus' criteria for greatness? It has been said that every relationship in life must be redemptive. This means that at the heart of that relationship, the Christian should always be seeking opportunities to help the other person come to know Christ or to grow in his relationship with Christ. This is the goal of serving—this is redemptive ministry.

One Sunday, my family and I were eating dinner when we heard someone on the roof of our house. I went outside to find one of the men of our church cleaning out the vent pipe that exited through the roof. That morning, I had casually mentioned to him that we had been having a plumbing problem. This friend had recognized an opportunity to serve. On another occasion, two fellow church members showed up at our house early one Saturday morning to replace the worn-out brakes on our car. I once returned home from a trip and discovered that another brother in the Lord had mowed our lawn. These small acts of kindness help strengthen relationships among Christians and serve as examples of redemptive ministry.

In what ways have you served others lately? Whether sharing the Gospel, visiting the sick, ministering to the poor, encouraging a fellow Christian, or some seemingly small act of kindness, there are countless ways in which we can follow Jesus' example. To put it another way, we should be engaged in a lifestyle of redemptive ministry.

It should be noted, however, that even service to others must not be at the exclusion of fulfilling our obligations to ourselves, our families, and any others who might be in our natural sphere of responsibility. We should serve people to please the Lord, not as they themselves might otherwise demand of us. We must serve where it can benefit Christ and His kingdom. We simply cannot be everything to everybody. One of our ongoing objectives as Christians should be to recognize how God is leading us into meaningful and effective Christian ministry.

Joseph W. Segree

An Unnatural Inversion

An unnatural inversion can be found in the program of God. According to Jesus, the first will be last and the last will be first. The one who loves his life will lose it, and the one who hates his life will keep it. In order to live, one must first die. He who humbles himself will be exalted. He who serves others will be exalted. Jesus is the supreme example of this inversion, but it can also be found in the Christian who follows that example. Jesus spoke of this inversion:

- "If anyone would come after me, he must deny himself and take up his cross and follow me. For whoever wants to save his life will lose it, but whoever loses his life for me will find it" (Matt. 16:24–25).
- "If anyone wants to be first, he must be the very last, and the servant of all. He took a little child and had him stand among them. Taking him in his arms, he said to them, 'Whoever welcomes one of these little children in my name welcomes me; and whoever welcomes me does not welcome me but the one who sent me'" (Mark 9:35–37).
- "The greatest among you will be your servant. For whoever exalts himself will be humbled, and whoever humbles himself will be exalted" (Matt. 23:11–12).
- "I tell you the truth, unless a kernel of wheat falls to the ground and dies, it remains only a single seed. But if it dies, it produces many seeds. The man who loves his life will lose it, while the man who hates his life in this world will keep it for eternal life. Whoever serves me must follow me; and where I am, my servant also will be. My Father will honor the one who serves me" (John 12:24–26).

In response to the disciples' dispute over greatness, Jesus said,

> The kings of the Gentiles lord it over them; and those who exercise authority over them call themselves Benefactors. But you are not to be like that. Instead, the greatest among you should be like the youngest, and the one who rules like the one who serves. For who is greater, the one who is at the table or the one who serves? Is it not the one who is at

the table? But I am among you as one who serves. (Luke 22:25–27)

And finally, when He had finished washing their feet, He put on His clothes, and returned to His place,

"Do you understand what I have done for you?" he asked them. "You call me 'Teacher' and 'Lord,' and rightly so, for that is what I am. Now that I, your Lord and Teacher, have washed your feet, you also should wash one another's feet. I have set you an example that you should do as I have done for you. I tell you the truth, no servant is greater than his master, nor is a messenger greater than the one who sent him." (John 13:12–16)

Jesus was a humble servant of God and of people. This is the biblical meaning of greatness!

CHAPTER 6

OUR SUPREME EXAMPLE

Greatness Embodied

> To the Son He says, "Your throne, O God, is forever
> and ever; a scepter of righteousness is the scepter of Your
> kingdom."
>
> —Hebrews 1:8 (NKJV)

In the previous chapters, we have seen greatness ascribed to a number of prominent characters in the Old Testament; bestowed upon God's servant John the Baptist; and achieved by the man Moses. We will now see it embodied by the very human person—Jesus Christ, the Son of God. In Romans 10:4, the apostle Paul says, "For Christ is the end of the law for righteousness to everyone who believes." In other words, our search for righteousness ends with Christ. We need to look no further. The same can be said of greatness. It ends with Christ. Do you want to achieve greatness in the biblical sense? Strive to be like Christ—He is our supreme model and example. Where He is—greatness is. Christ *is* greatness!

Jesus's life has been called the most attractive, noble, courageous, and beautiful life ever lived. As with every human virtue, He was the embodiment of greatness! He served not just by healing people—and not just by the supreme act of dying for our sins—but through countless acts of kindness. He provided wine at the wedding in Cana and broke bread at the Last Supper. He cooked breakfast by the Sea of Galilee and served it to His disciples. In the seemingly small things of life, He served. One can imagine Jesus giving His cloak to a disciple who complained about being cold, gathering wood for a fire, and sharing his food with a beggar. In innumerable ways, the Son of God served people during His brief earthly life.

That life began in a stable and ended on a Roman cross. Jesus owned no earthly possessions except the clothes He wore. He often associated with outcasts, outsiders, and outlaws. He touched lepers, talked with those who were demon possessed, preached to the poor, ate with publicans, and died between thieves. Apart from sin, Jesus knew the entire range of human infirmities: hunger, thirst, fatigue, weariness, grief, loneliness, mockery, ridicule, temptation, and so forth. By such complete identification with the human race, He could say, "Come to Me, all who are weary and heavy-laden, and I will give you rest. Take My yoke upon you and learn from Me, for I am gentle and humble in heart, and you will find rest for your souls. For My yoke is easy and My burden is light" (Matt. 11:28–30).

Jesus did not select influential or highly educated men but ordinary ones as His closest followers. He hung out with people who would never be considered important. He did not teach and preach to impress anyone but to reveal the will of His Father in heaven. He avoided publicity and often tried to evade the crowds, though they still thronged about Him.

In his book *Jesus the Revolutionary*, H.S. Vigiveno describes Jesus' humility:

> He calls no attention to Himself with a voice blaring from heaven over a celestial loudspeaker. God announces Himself to a teenage girl, is born as a little baby, and hardly anybody pays attention. He begins helping nobodies in the forgotten part of the Roman Empire. He has time for women and children, and lays His hands on miserable people who live in dirty places. He arrives, telling us that God's kingdom is like a hidden treasure. He enters Jerusalem on a donkey. The heroes of the world come on horses. They are men of war. He comes on a beast of burden, symbolizing peace.
>
> The proud rulers of the world are surrounded by weapons of war. Jesus has only palm branches around Him. Most rulers come well protected by police and secret service men. He arrives unprotected. He comes humbly. And when the parade thins and the shouting dies down, He seems to slip away. He gets lost among the temple crowd.[1]

The writer goes on to say that if Jesus had come striding through the world as some Messianic king, we could never get close to Him. We could only wave and admire Him. But we can get close to Him because He humbled Himself, became a man, and allowed Himself to be humiliated on a cross.

> He was oppressed and He was afflicted, yet He did not open His mouth; like a lamb that is led to slaughter, and like a sheep that is silent before its shearers, so He did not open His mouth. He was oppressed and afflicted, yet he did not open his mouth; he was led like a lamb to the slaughter, and as a sheep before her shearers is silent, so he did not open his mouth. (Isa. 53:7)

We see Jesus' humility even after His resurrection. Instead of coming as a victorious king, announced by heavenly trumpeters, He met His disciples quietly at breakfast, which He had prepared for them by the seashore—always serving (John 21). He who was Master became servant. He who was somebody became nobody. He who was life died. This is what it means to be humble. But nowhere is His greatness seen more—this humility and serving—than on the cross, where He submitted to the will of God and in shame, suffering, and disgrace served all humanity by dying for our sins. He did not insist upon His position with His heavenly Father but willingly gave it up to become a human being. How different from emperors and dictators, who often claimed to be gods.

Paul describes the greatness of Jesus Christ in these incomparable words:

> Have this attitude in yourselves which was also in Christ Jesus, who, although He existed in the form of God, did not regard equality with God a thing to be grasped, but emptied Himself, taking the form of a bond-servant, and being made in the likeness of men. Being found in appearance as a man, He humbled Himself by becoming obedient to the point of death, even death on a cross. For this reason also, God highly exalted Him, and bestowed on Him the name which is above every name, so that at the name of Jesus every knee will bow, of those who are in

heaven and on earth and under the earth, and that every tongue will confess that Jesus Christ is Lord, to the glory of God the Father. (Phil. 2:5–11)

Again quoting the prophet Isaiah,

Behold, My Servant, whom I uphold; My chosen one in whom My soul delights. I have put My Spirit upon Him; He will bring forth justice to the nations. He will not cry out or raise His voice, nor make His voice heard in the street. A bruised reed He will not break and a dimly burning wick He will not extinguish; He will faithfully bring forth justice. He will not be disheartened or crushed until He has established justice in the earth; and the coastlands will wait expectantly for His Law. (Isa. 42:1–4)

This embodiment of greatness has been eloquently expressed in the popular poem "One Solitary Life" by James Allen Francis:

More than nineteen hundred years ago, there was a Man born contrary to the laws of life. This Man lived in poverty and was reared in obscurity. He did not travel extensively. Only once did He cross the boundary of the country in which He lived; that was during His exile in childhood. He possessed neither wealth nor influence. His relatives were inconspicuous and had neither training nor formal education. In infancy He startled a king; in childhood He puzzled doctors; in manhood He ruled the course of nature, walked upon the waves as pavement, and hushed the sea to sleep.

He healed the multitudes without medicine and made no charge for His service. He never wrote a book, and yet perhaps all the libraries of the world could not hold the books that have been written about Him. He never wrote a song, and yet He has furnished the theme for more songs than all the songwriters combined. He never founded a college, but all the schools put together cannot boast of having as many students. He never marshaled an army, nor drafted a soldier, nor fired a gun; and yet no leader ever had more volunteers who have, under His orders, made more rebels stack arms and surrender without a shot fired.

He never practiced psychiatry, and yet He has healed more broken hearts than all the doctors far and near. Once each week multitudes congregate at worshiping assemblies to pay homage and respect to Him. The names of the past, proud statesmen of Greece and Rome have come and gone. The names of the past scientists, philosophers, and theologians have come and gone. But the name of this Man multiplies more and more. Though time has spread nineteen hundred years between the people of this generation and the mockers at His crucifixion, He still lives. His enemies could not destroy Him, and the grave could not hold Him. He stands forth upon the highest pinnacle of heavenly glory, proclaimed of God, acknowledged by angels, adored by saints, and feared by devils, as the risen, personal Christ, our Lord and Savior.[2]

CHAPTER 7

GREATNESS EXHORTED

A Preeminent Goal

"For we do not preach ourselves but Christ Jesus as Lord,
and ourselves as your bond-servants for Jesus' sake."
—2 Corinthians 4:5

There is no shortage of stories about humility in the journals of well-known people. Walter Cronkite recalls the following incident:

> Sailing back down the Mystic River in Connecticut and following the channel's tricky turns through an expanse of shallow water, I am reminded of the time a boatload of young people sped past us here, its occupants shouting and waving their arms. I waved back a cheery greeting and my wife said, "Do you know what they were shouting?"
> "Why, it was 'Hello, Walter,'" I replied. "No," she said. "They were shouting, 'Low water, Low water.'" Such are the pitfalls of fame's egotism.[1]

Nobody whom Jesus healed ever went away proclaiming his own greatness. While some may not have stopped to give thanks (nine of the ten lepers in Luke 17), they must nevertheless have experienced an overwhelming sense of humility before the one who healed them. Nothing humbles a person quite like a direct encounter with the living God! Many of us who know Christ personally have had our own burning bush experience—maybe not as dramatic as that of Moses but nevertheless as real and life-changing. And with this new awareness of spiritual reality comes a sense of our own unworthiness before God.

Yet from the very moment of conversion, there is planted in the heart of every believer the seeds of sanctification. While the word *sanctification* has several theological applications, it is used here to represent the journey toward Christlikeness that each of us experiences. It is a lifelong process, a quest for holiness brought about in the believer by obedience to Christ and His Word. Can total absolute Christlikeness be attained in this life? No. Neither can absolute humility and servanthood, perhaps, but its attainment can and should be sought.

George Washington Carver, the scientist who developed hundreds of useful products from the peanut, gave this testimony:

When I was young, I said to God, "God, tell me the mystery of the universe."

But God answered, "That knowledge is reserved for me alone."

So I said, "God, tell me the mystery of the peanut."

Then God said, "Well, George, that's more nearly your size." And he told me.[2]

The biblical meaning of greatness, defined by Jesus as humility and servanthood, can also be found in the New Testament epistles. Paul is a leading example of one who exhorted others to pursue biblical greatness, while exhibiting it himself. He was on a mission to Damascus to persecute Christians when he was confronted by Jesus Christ. Blinded by a dazzling light and stunned by a voice from heaven, he was brought to his knees by the power and presence of the Lord (Acts 9). Paul soon realized that he had been mistaken about the resurrection of Jesus of Nazareth and about those who were called Christians. Jesus was, in truth, the Messiah, and Paul's vehement persecution of those who confessed Him was a heinous sin.

His humility and servant spirit are evident in the accounts of his missionary journeys recorded in the Acts of the Apostles, as well as in certain sections of his epistles (2 Cor. 11 and 12). Consider the following words of the New Testament writers regarding humility and servanthood:

- Paul wrote, "But he who boasts is to boast in the LORD, for it is not he who commends himself that is approved, but he whom the Lord commends" (2 Cor. 10:17–18).

- After describing the many hardships he had undergone for the sake of the Gospel, Paul concludes, "If I have to boast, I will boast of what pertains to my Weakness" (2 Cor. 11:30).
- Continuing Paul's exhortations, "And He has said to me, 'My grace is sufficient for you, for power is perfected in weakness.' Most gladly, therefore, I will rather boast about my weaknesses, so that the power of Christ may dwell in me. Therefore I am well content with weaknesses, with insults, with distresses, with persecutions, with difficulties, for Christ's sake; for when I am weak, then I am strong" (2 Cor. 12:9–10).
- "For we do not preach ourselves but Christ Jesus as Lord, and ourselves as your bond-servants for Jesus' sake" (2 Cor. 4:5).
- Addressing the elders of the church in Ephesus, Paul said, "Serving the Lord with all humility and with tears and with trials which came upon me through the plots of the Jews" (Acts 20:19).

When Paul, in his thirteen epistles, speaks of humility and service to others, he is doing so out of the depths of his own experience:

- "The things you have learned and received and heard and seen in me, practice these things, and the God of peace will be with you" (Phil. 4:9).
- "With all humility and gentleness, with patience, showing tolerance for one another in love" (Eph. 4:2).
- "Be subject to one another in the fear of Christ" (Eph. 5:21).
- "So, as those who have been chosen of God, holy and beloved, put on a heart of compassion, kindness, humility, gentleness and patience" (Col. 3:12).
- "Remind them to be subject to rulers, to authorities, to be obedient, to be ready for every good deed, to malign no one, to be peaceable, gentle, showing every consideration for all men" (Titus 3:1–2).
- "Be of the same mind toward one another; do not be haughty in mind, but associate with the lowly. Do not be wise in your own estimation" (Rom. 12:16).
- "Not lagging behind in diligence, fervent in spirit, serving the Lord" (Rom. 12:11).

- "For you were called to freedom, brethren; only do not turn your freedom into an opportunity for the flesh, but through love serve one another" (Gal. 5:13).
- "For though I am free from all men, I have made myself a slave to all, so that I may win more" (1 Cor. 9:19).

James, the brother of Jesus and leader of the early Jerusalem church, wrote about humility:

> But he gives us more grace. That is why Scripture says: "But He gives a greater grace." Therefore it says, "God is opposed to the proud, but gives grace to the humble." Submit therefore to God. Resist the devil and he will flee from you. Humble yourselves in the presence of the Lord, and He will exalt you. (James 4:6–7, 10)

Also Peter, who probably observed Jesus' life as closely as any other human being, said the following:

- "As each one has received a special gift, employ it in serving one another as good stewards of the manifold grace of God" (1 Peter 4:10).
- "Shepherd the flock of God among you, exercising oversight not under compulsion, but voluntarily, according to the will of God; and not for sordid gain, but with eagerness" (1 Peter 5:2).
- "You younger men, likewise, be subject to your elders; and all of you, clothe yourselves with humility toward one another, for God is opposed to the proud but gives grace to the humble. Therefore humble yourselves under the mighty hand of God, that He may exalt you at the proper time" (1 Peter 5:5–6).

Finally, consider the words of the apostle John:

- "Therefore be imitators of God, as beloved children; and walk in love, just as Christ also loved you and gave Himself up for us, an offering and a sacrifice to God as a fragrant aroma" (1 John 5:2).
- "We know love by this, that He laid down His life for us; and we ought to lay down our lives for the brethren. But whoever has

the world's goods, and sees his brother in need and closes his heart against him, how does the love of God abide in him? Little children, let us not love with word or with tongue, but in deed and truth" (1 John 3:16–18).

Thus, the meaning of greatness can be seen throughout the New Testament. Whenever we are exhorted to imitate God or to be like Christ, we are being called to greatness. If you want to be called great in the kingdom of God—if you want to be His disciple—you must be a humble servant of the Lord Jesus Christ.

NOTES

Chapter 1
1   The Apostolic Benediction: 2 Corinthians 13:14.
2   This prayer is quoted from a sermon by Ray Stedman, "The Greatness of God," September 3, 1967 (Ray Stedman Ministries, Palo Alto, California).

Chapter 2
1   Asceticism refers to the practice of strict self-denial as a means of religious discipline.

Chapter 3
1   The Levitical priesthood began with Aaron, the older brother of Moses, and included his descendants. These Levites (from the tribe of Levi) served as the priests in Israel, ministering in the tabernacle and later the temple, primarily as mediators between man and God.

Chapter 4
1   Jesus performed nature miracles when He walked on water, calmed a storm, turned water into wine, multiplied the fish and the loaves, and other such things.

Chapter 5
1   C.J. Mahaney, *Humility: True Greatness* (Colorado Springs, CO: Multnomah Books, 2005).
2   Dwight Hill, *Facts of the Matter* (Auburn CA: Global Marketplace Initiative, 2003).
3   Source unknown.
4   Andrew Murray, *Humility* (New York: Anson D. F. Randolph and Company, 1895).

Chapter 6

1   Hugh Vigeveno, *Jesus the Revolutionary* (Glendale, CA: Regal Books, 1966), 144.
2   James Allan Francis (1864–1928), *One Solitary Life*.

Chapter 7

1   From Ray Ellis and Walter Cronkite, *North by Northeast*.
2   Source unknown.

BOOK 3

Life in the Marketplace

A Biblical View of Man's Work and Ministry

CONTENTS

"The sun rises ... then man goes out to his
work, to his labor until evening."
—Psalm 104:22–23

INTRODUCTION

We are often known by our vocations, as understood by such frequently asked questions as "What line of work are you in?" and "What do you do for a living?" People judge us on the basis of how we earn a living, sometimes drawing conclusions about such things as our education, income, lifestyle, and social status. Few things are as important as our work, for this is how we spend the majority of our waking hours, earn our income, and contribute to the society in which we live.

For Christians, however, there is another issue involved. God calls us to serve others and to minister to people, regardless of how we earn a living. We therefore have a responsibility toward our coworkers and associates, as well as toward others we encounter in the workplace.

Men often face tough questions when they come into a saving relationship with Jesus Christ, especially if they have a strong desire to minister to others. "Should I view my work differently now that I am a follower of Christ? Can I still be content in my present career? Is it possible to integrate my work and ministry in such a way as to find fulfillment in both? Will God really use me at work to make a difference in people's lives, or should I consider going into the ministry?" This book answers these and related questions. I am convinced that God's primary plan for most men is to minister in the marketplace, where we work and interact with other people in the ordinary affairs of life.

The purpose of this book is to present a brief biblical view of this vital subject as I understand it and hopefully to help equip the reader to represent the Lord Jesus Christ more effectively in the workplace.

CHAPTER 1

A DIVINE COMMAND

Labor is an expression of God's grace. Work is the means by which God wants us to occupy our time in the perfection of His creation plan. When God created Adam, He "took the man and put him in the Garden of Eden to work it and take care of it" (Gen. 2:15). King Solomon wrote, "A man can do nothing better than to eat and drink and find satisfaction in his work. This too, I see, is from the hand of God" (Eccl. 2:24).

The apostle Paul, chosen by God to be a missionary to the Gentiles, was an evangelist and a church founder. He wrote much of the New Testament, yet Paul was also a man who worked with his hands in a useful trade: "And because he was a tentmaker as they were, he stayed and worked with them" (Acts 18:3). He wrote to the Thessalonians,

> For you yourselves know how you ought to follow our example. We were not idle when we were with you, nor did we eat anyone's food without paying for it. On the contrary, we worked night and day, laboring and toiling so that we would not be a burden to any of you. We did this, not because we do not have the right to such help, but in order to make ourselves a model for you to follow. For even when we were with you, we gave you this rule: "If a man will not work, he shall not eat." (2 Thess. 3:7–10)

It is universally accepted that we must work in order to eat and acquire the other necessities of life. Jesus Himself was a working man, and He called twelve working men to be His first disciples. However, He did not

109

demand that others who accepted Him give up their work, not even a notorious tax collector by the name of Zacchaeus (Luke 19:1–10),John the Baptist approved the work of tax collectors when he exhorted them to collect no more than was due. He also recognized the military profession by telling soldiers to be content with their pay (Luke 3:12–14).

According to the Bible, then, the first reason we work is because God commanded it, but not just for the purpose of earning a living. God has already promised that He will provide us with the necessities of life. On the subject of food, drink, and clothing, Jesus said, "Your heavenly Father knows that you need them. But seek first His kingdom and His righteousness, and all these things will be given to you as well" (Matt. 6:32–33).God can provide for us apart from our work, if He chooses to do so. In other words, work plays a much greater role in our lives than just a means of acquiring food, clothing, and shelter.

Imagine, for example, a pioneer family dwelling in the wilderness. The father instructs his son, "Your job for the next few weeks will be to cut wood in the forest. This will require great effort and will occupy most of your waking hours. I want you to sell the wood or trade with the men who are building the town, as well as other settlers in the community."

The son responds agreeably, "I understand, Father. You want me to work to help support our family."

"Not entirely," says the father. "I will provide for you and for the others in our family. he money you earn will help, of course, but the responsibility to provide is mine, not yours."

Now the son is certain that there will be plenty to eat because his father has promised to provide, yet he knows that, to some degree, his own labor will go toward that end. "Very well, Father," the young man replies. "I will do as you say."

Just as the father, not the son, provides for the family, God provides us with the necessities of life, and our work will most often be His primary means of doing this.

The second reason we work is to be in an environment where we can represent Jesus Christ. The workplace has been called the "nine-to-five window." It is not just a place to perform meaningful labor but an environment for ministry. Not only are we to *work* as unto the Lord—we must also *minister* as unto the Lord.

Opportunities for ministry will be as diverse as the marketplace*itself. Some workers—store clerks, for example—encounter many people each day, while others, such as farmers or construction workers, may come into contact with very few.

Writing in defense of his ministry, Paul said, "We, however, will not boast beyond proper limits, but will confine our boasting to the field God has assigned to us" (2 Cor. 10:13). God has assigned each of us a field of labor, a sphere of influence that includes our work environment. As we minister in the workplace, our ultimate goal is to help people come to know Jesus Christ as Savior and Lord and to help them grow in their relationship with Him.

God means for us to find contentment in our labor. To do this, we must view God as our boss and strive to please Him through our work. If we are business owners, we must relinquish ownership to God. Here is our guiding principle: "Whatever you do, work at it with all your heart, as working for the Lord, not for men, since you know that you will receive an inheritance from the Lord as a reward. It is the Lord Christ you are serving" (Col. 3:23–24).

The US Army once had a recruiting slogan that said, "Be all that you can be." When a young man accepted a position with a new company, his father's advice was simple: "Make them glad they hired you." As a teenage left for summer camp, her mother counseled her, "Remember your name," reminding her not to do anything that would reflect poorly upon the family. These expressions should describe our attitude as we represent the Lord Jesus Christ in the workplace. We should be the best we can be—an asset to the company and determined never to bring discredit upon the Lord.

A biblical view of work, one that should motivate us to work "as unto the Lord," includes an eternal perspective. At the funeral of a well-known billionaire, a young man asked, "How much did he leave?" Someone replied, "All of it, son. He left all of it."

We all agree that we cannot take our money or material possessions with us when we die. When we begin to follow Christ, we discover that we cannot achieve a true sense of fulfillment and significance through material wealth or through any temporal, worldly labor. At best, work can provide only temporary satisfaction and contentment. Since God created us for eternity, real significance can be found only in His Son, Jesus Christ. Jesus said, "I have come that they may have life, and that they may have it more abundantly" (John 10:10 NKJV). This abundant life that Jesus promises comes only through a right relationship with Him.

Our goal on the job should not be to make as much money as possible, achieve the highest standard of living, or become the president of the company. Our goal must be to represent Christ! "We are therefore Christ's ambassadors, as though God were making his appeal through us.We implore you on Christ's behalf: Be reconciled to God" (2 Cor.5:20). If our focus is on the wrong thing, our commitment to Christ can be negatively influenced and our witness compromised.

A biblical view of man and his work also includes the idea of separation. The Bible says, "Therefore come out from them and be separate, says the Lord" (2 Cor. 6:17). Christians are admonished not to indulge in the ungodly attitudes, philosophies, and ways of the world. We are *in* the world but not *of* the world. We are to be separated *to* God, not separated *from* people. How can we minister to people if we do not engage them in the affairs of life?

According to J. Allan Petersen, "We must deliberately seek the place where the crowded ways of life merge and then sing, 'In the cross of Christ I glory.' That is the place of danger, but it is the place our Lord wants us to be—as sheep in the midst of wolves. Only when we are in that place shall we be able to fulfill our commission: 'As the Father hath sent me, even so send I you.'" [1]

Marketplace is used here to refer to the whole arena of jobs and places where people work, while *workplace* represents a person's specific place of employment.

CHAPTER 2

A MATTER OF FUNDING

"It was he who gave some to be apostles, some to be prophets, some to be evangelists, and some to be pastors and teachers, to prepare God's people for works of service, so that the body of Christ may be built up" (Eph. 4:11–12). Simply stated, "works of service" refer to activities directed toward bringing people into a saving relationship with Jesus Christ and helping to build them up in the Christian faith.[1] This service (ministry) must be distinguished from purely religious or even church activity, though it may be a part of both. To minister is to be in the service of the Lord Jesus Christ—to be a participant in His work of redemption.[2]

The equipping ministers mentioned in Ephesians 4:11, ordained and appointed by the head of the church, Jesus Christ Himself, can be seen in various New Testament passages. For example, "Now we ask you, brothers, to respect those who work hard among you, who are over you in the Lord and who admonish you. Hold them in the highest regard in love because of their work. Live in peace with each other" (1 Thess. 5:12–13). In his letters to Timothy and Titus, Paul exhorts them to respect the pastoral office, as does the writer of Hebrews (Heb. 13:17).

Thus, we see within the church two categories of ministers functioning in a complementary fashion: (1) those specially called to equip others for ministry; and (2) those who would be equipped to carry out ministry—that is, the rank and file of the church. Ministry is every believer's responsibility. By means of God-given gifts, such as preaching, teaching, encouraging, giving, and leading, the body of Christ is edified. One church expressed this biblical view when it posted the following notice on a billboard:

MINISTERS—ALL OF THE MEMBERS
ASSISTANT TO THE MINISTERS—THE PASTOR

In the modern church, there is another classification of ministers, one best described by the term *vocational*. This classification is based upon how these ministers derive their living. It consists of those who obtain their income solely or largely from the work of the ministry, as distinct from those whose livelihood comes through some other vocation. Though many are called to serve as vocational ministers, as Christians, we are each called to serve according to the gifts, abilities, and opportunities that God has given us.

How did this distinction between vocational and non-vocational ministers come into existence? Some understanding of the priesthood is necessary to answer this question. In Genesis 4:3–5, both Cain and Abel functioned in the capacity of a priest in that each was responsible for his own offering to God. Likewise, "Noah built an altar to the LORD and, taking some of all the clean animals and clean birds, he sacrificed burnt offerings on it" (Gen. 8:20). Abraham, as well as his sons and grandsons, repeatedly offered sacrifices to God. Originally then, every individual functioned as his own priest before God.

When Moses, after leading the Hebrews out of Egypt, went up onto Mt. Sinai to receive the Law, God gave him instructions to form a "professional priesthood." God appointed the tribe of Levi to serve as priests and ministers (Exod. 28–29 and Num. 3). The book of Hebrews tells us that the sacrificial system was a preview of the cross, where the sacrifice of Jesus Christ would once and for all provide the pardon for man's sin, thus ending the Levitical order of priests. In the New Testament, both Peter and John declare all believers to be priests: "But you are a chosen people, a royal priesthood, a holy nation, a people belonging to God" (1 Peter 2:9). "Jesus has made us to be a kingdom and priests to serve his God and Father—to Him be glory and power forever and ever! Amen" (Rev. 1:6). (A distinction must be made between the term *priests* as it is used by the New Testament writers as opposed to its meaning with respect to Anglican, Eastern Orthodox, and Roman Catholic clergymen. This latter usage is neither found nor implied in this book.)

Historically then, until the time of Moses and God's giving of the Law, each person was responsible for functioning as a priest before God. Then, for approximately fifteen hundred years until Christ appeared on earth, the professional priesthood existed. At the death of Christ, the church reverted to the former days of the priesthood of the believers. Each believer is now free to approach the throne of God, as well as to serve as a minister of God. "Let us then approach the throne of grace with confidence, so that we may receive mercy and find grace to help us in our time of need" (Heb. 4:16).

Although church officers (bishops and deacons) are mentioned in the New Testament, no priesthood can be found apart from the priesthood of the believer. No office can usurp from the believer his right and responsibility to serve as a minister of God. This right of the individual believer, through the use of spiritual gifts, became the driving force of the New Testament Church. The early church recognized no class distinction between its officers and all other believers.[3]

Sometime after the earliest years of the church, the word *minister* moved both grammatically and theologically from a verb (a thing done) to a noun (a person doing it). What was originally a *function of* the church became a *station in* the church. Ministry was originally the assignment of all believers, but somehow it became limited to the professionals, resulting in a radical and far-reaching change in the church. The practice of church government, rather than the exercise of spiritual gifts, began to prevail more and more. Eventually, there came into existence a sharply defined distinction between the religious professionals and the ordinary members of the local church body. As the Christian community expanded, there came a desire to establish a full-time professional ministry to manage and oversee the growing church. More and more, the church began to structure itself on the basis of the former Levitical order, rather than on the purely New Testament idea of every person a priest.

As the first century came to a close, a new word was introduced into the church—*clergy*. The term came to be applied distinctively to the professional ministry. What is perhaps the most striking thing about this separation between the clergy and other members of the church is that, in spite of centuries of tradition and teaching to the contrary, there is no biblical basis for it. It may be impossible, however, to eradicate the perception that the ministry, for the most part, should be left up to the professionals. Many Christians simply do not see themselves as accountable to God for ministering to people. Satan has managed to preserve this error in the church for centuries, preventing many from having any significant involvement in the advancement of the kingdom of God.

This universal Christian responsibility for ministry can be illustrated as follows: In most wars, there exist side by side two groups of combatants, both committed to the cause for which they fight. The first group is comprised of professional soldiers who wear uniforms and get paid for their services. The second group is made up of those belonging to the resistance or underground—people who earn their living in some way other than as soldiers and who blend in with their surroundings. A friend of mine, while speaking at a gathering of Christian optometrists on the subject of ministering in the workplace, referred to himself as "a soldier of Jesus Christ cleverly disguised as an optometrist." As laymen committed to Jesus Christ, we must work undercover in whatever disguise our jobs call for, being largely unrecognizable as ministers of the Gospel. Yet we can be actively sharing Christ through the opportunities that arise in the workplace environment. The clergyman says, "My ministry is my work," while the layman says, "My work is my ministry."

For many, there is the perception that lay people are the normal Christians, while the professionals are the *called ones*—those who possess some greater spirituality or devotion to God. Martin Luther, the great sixteenth-century reformer, insisted that the public ministry was simply a matter of practical function or vocation, not a higher or more religious form of life with a special standing in God's eyes. We are all saved through faith by the grace of God and are called to live in obedience to Christ. This is the normal Christian life. Again, it has nothing to do with vocation. Some earn their living through Christian vocations, while most of us work in *regular* or *secular* jobs.

The common expression "full-time Christian service" is misleading, for it contributes to the perception that Christian ministry must be distinct from the ordinary affairs of life. While God does call people into vocational Christian ministry, He also directs Christians into other areas of work. He expects us to work and, at the same time, to impact the world for Jesus Christ. Our primary ministry should not necessarily take place in the church building on Sundays and Wednesdays, or even through church programs and activities, but in the workplace.

Similarly, the concept of *bi-vocational* ministry may be misleading. Consider, for example, the man who works in an office five days a week and also serves as pastor of a church. He is bi-vocational in the sense that he has two vocations: his office work and his church work. But this does not mean that he is a minister only at church. He is not a minister because he is a pastor; he is a pastor because he is a minister. He is a minister because he is a follower of Jesus Christ, regardless of how he earns his living.

Fundamental to both the vocational and the non-vocational minister is the issue of money. The vocational Christian worker gets paid for doing the ministry, while the layman derives his living in some other way. Thus, as ministers of the Gospel, we differ in this one essential way—where our pay comes from. In the end, it is just a matter of funding.

CHAPTER 3

THE PEOPLE BUSINESS

Missionary life in Calcutta, India, would be quite different from that in inner-city Chicago, La Paz, Bolivia, or the jungles of Papua New Guinea. Missionaries have to be uniquely qualified to serve in such diverse settings around the world. This diversity can be seen in the environment, climate, culture, race, language, religion, and other regional characteristics.

There is also great diversity in the mission field known as *the marketplace*. Work environments differ in countless ways: a corporate executive's office, a factory, a construction site, a hospital, an elementary school, a department store, a restaurant, and so forth. For those whose jobs bring them into contact with the public, there are frequent encounters with new people, while others associate with the same people every day. In some situations, workers can talk freely, yet in others, this is almost impossible. Some people spend most of the workday alone, while many are never alone. But regardless of our particular work environment, as Christians, we are, in a sense, in the same business—the people business.

Ministry may be defined as "specialized, concentrated activities or actions carried out in the name of Jesus Christ by groups or individuals utilizing God-given gifts, natural talents, or acquired skills to (a) serve people in need; (b) influence unbelievers toward salvation; and (c) encourage Christians toward spiritual maturity."[1] Although our methods and techniques for ministry may vary, certain principles apply no matter what our work environment might be. This chapter offers some guidelines and suggestions for ministering effectively on the job.

In the workplace, as everywhere else, we must "live the Christian Life." Jesus said, "You are the salt of the earth ... You are the light of the world"

(Matt. 5:13–14). Jesus used salt and light to illustrate the effect that our lives should have upon other people. Just as salt is an appetizer, the quality of our lives should be appealing to those who observe us. We should strive to be above reproach in our speech, attitudes, and actions. "As a prisoner for the Lord, then, I urge you to live a life worthy of the calling you have received" (Eph. 4:1). In the same way that light shines from a lamp, the truth of the Gospel must shine forth from our lives for people to see—first as we strive to imitate Christ and then as we share the message of salvation.

We cannot minister effectively in Jesus' name unless we are living in obedience to the Word of God. One reason for this is that people are quick to recognize a difference between what we say and what we do. Actions speak louder than words. If we act one way and talk another, people will always assume that the actions represent the real truth about us. Another reason why *living the life* is so important is that disobedience, even so-called little sins, grieves God, quenches the Spirit, and deprives us of God's power to work. "And do not grieve the Holy Spirit of God" (Eph. 4:30). "Do not put out the Spirit's fire" (1 Thess. 5:19).

Needy people are all around us. "Do you not say, 'Four months more and then the harvest'? I tell you, open your eyes and look at the fields! They are ripe for harvest" (John 4:35). Christ calls us to be a priesthood of believers who willingly take responsibility for ministering to those around us. We need to work with our eyes and ears open in order to recognize opportunities for ministry. Christ uses believers as His representatives, or agents, in sharing His love, compassion, and wisdom. As we labor in the marketplace, we will observe an unending array of human needs: a man with a terminal illness; a woman suffering the pain of divorce or grieving over the death of a loved one; a man who has lost his job and is facing serious financial difficulties; a person living with discouragement or depression; a couple struggling with a problem teenager; an elderly woman with failing health and a fear of death; an accident victim living with pain; a single person dealing with loneliness; people who feel unloved or uncared for; and so forth. They all need a listening ear and words of kindness from someone who genuinely cares about them. Most importantly, though, they need to know about the love of Jesus Christ and His power to change their lives.

Believers and unbelievers alike should be the objects of Christian ministry. We must be prepared to share the Gospel with people who have not heard or understood it, yet also be ready to serve our brothers and sisters in Christ. Paul exhorted the Thessalonians to comfort and edify one another, to uphold the weak, to rejoice and pray for one another, and much more (1 Thess. 5:11–14). Even in the workplace, we can look for ways to minister to both groups.

We can minister most effectively through human relationships. "So, affectionately longing for you, we were well pleased to impart to you not only the gospel of God, but also our own lives, because you had become dear to us" (1 Thess. 2:8). Inside every person there is a desire to be wanted, needed, and fulfilled. The thing that best satisfies these deep longings is a relationship with Jesus Christ. Thus, our ultimate goal in ministry is to help people come to know Christ and grow in their union with Him. In order to do this, it is often necessary first to get to know people, thereby opening doors of opportunity for ministry. Some of the things that can lead to meaningful relationships are genuine friendliness, listening to what people have to say (especially about their problems and concerns), showing a sincere interest in others, and performing acts of kindness. A deep or longstanding relationship is seldom necessary; otherwise, we could minister only to our close friends and family members.

In the case of unbelievers, the goal is to gain opportunities to share Christ. What may begin with casual conversation in the workplace could lead to a discussion in the coffee shop about the Bible or sharing a personal testimony on the golf course. By whatever means possible, an intermediate goal should be to gain a person's confidence in order to engage him with an evangelical witness. A relationship of some kind is also helpful in ministering to fellow Christians.

People must hear about Christ in order to believe in Him. "How, then, can they call on the one they have not believed in? And how can they believe in the one of whom they have not heard? And how can they hear without someone preaching to them?" (Rom.10:14). "Consequently, faith comes from hearing the message, and the message is heard through the word of Christ" (Rom. 10:17).

There are many ways by which a person can be exposed to the Gospel: from the words of a preacher or Bible teacher; by reading the Bible or an evangelistic Gospel tract; by listening to someone share how he got saved; by attending a Christian musical or dramatic event; and so forth. In any case, for people to be saved, they must first understand the Gospel message. As noted previously, we must develop relationships while living lives that conform to biblical standards, but unless we tell people how they can know Christ, nobody will be saved. Nobody ever went to heaven simply by observing the exemplary life of some Christian friend or acquaintance. There must also have been a clear communication of the Gospel.

After making a decision to follow Christ, a man was congratulated by his boss. "Are you a Christian?" the employee asked.

"Oh yes," replied the senior man. "I've been a Christian for twenty-three years."

"I have always known you to be a fair, considerate, and honest man," said the other. "If you had told me about Christ, I might have accepted Him long ago!"

We will probably never know how many people have been lost to the kingdom of God because we failed to tell them about our own relationship with Christ and about how they too could have eternal life. Consider your own work environment. You can take a mental survey of your coworkers, noting your impression as to those who seem to be Christians and others who do not. Then pray about how you can best approach them, asking God to show you how to encourage the believers and how to tell the unbelievers about Jesus.

Ministry begins when we identify a need in someone's life and initiate some course of action. More often than not, this action involves talking to the person and then deciding how we can help him. If the ministry involves sharing the Gospel, there may be some anxiety or fear to overcome, but this usually disappears once we begin to talk about Jesus Christ and spiritual things.

Start by listening and looking for some common ground for interaction. Focus on a person's interests or on some obvious area of need. Ask key questions to turn the conversation toward spiritual matters: "Are you interested in spiritual things?" "Do you believe in God?" "Do you attend church?" "Do you ever read the Bible?" Be a little bold in your effort to connect with him on spiritual matters. Give him an appropriate Gospel tract or a pocket-sized, contemporary translation of the New Testament. Ask him if there is some matter that you can pray about for him. In some cases, you may be able to encourage him right then and there, share with him a word of testimony, or invite him to Bible study or church. In other instances, you may need to follow up at some more opportune time. But remember—ministry to unbelievers should always include, as its foremost objective, a clear presentation of the Gospel of Jesus Christ.

Support your ministry with prayer. "Devote yourselves to prayer, being watchful and thankful. And pray for us, too, that God may open a door for our message, so that we may proclaim the mystery of Christ, for which I am in chains" (Col. 4:2–3). As a young Christian, Dawson Trotman, founder of the Navigators, would often begin his day with this simple prayer: "Lord, we're just reporting for duty. We don't know who we'll meet today or what their need will be, but give us the right word for them."[2]

The following prayer further illustrates the essential role of prayer in ministry:

> Heavenly Father, I am going into my mission field today looking for opportunities to minister to people in the name of Jesus Christ. Grant me the discernment to recognize these opportunities, the wisdom to respond to them properly, and the faith to trust You to work in the lives of people I meet. Let me be salt and light so that they might be drawn to Christ through my life. Cause me to speak the right words at the right time and in the right way. In Jesus name I pray. Amen.[2]

CHAPTER 4

BALANCE AND PERSPECTIVE

Although God commands us to work, He does not mean for us to give our lives to our jobs. Though work may consume a large portion of our time, it must not consume us. As noted previously, we labor (1) because God commands it; (2) in order to make our lives more meaningful; and (3) because of the ministry we can perform. But work must be in balance with the other areas of our lives. We must devote the proper time and attention to family and home responsibilities, church, health, and personal interests. Excessive attention to work can crowd these other important areas of our lives and keep us from meeting our God-given responsibilities. This also applies to vocational ministers. A pastor has the same responsibility as any other man toward his family and the other areas of his life. It is doubtful that any man, just before dying, ever wished that he had spent more time on the job. Failure to meet these obligations reflects a life that is out of balance.

During the five years that I spent in the army, I wore my uniform only when I was on duty; otherwise, I wore civilian clothes. I was frequently away from the army post, not engaged in military affairs or activities. Yet during that period, there was never a moment when I was not a soldier. The uniform did not make me a soldier, nor did my surroundings or activities. I was a soldier because of an oath I had taken to serve in the army.

We cannot compartmentalize our lives. The areas of our lives will always overlap. We are working men wherever we might be: on the job, at church, at the ballgame, or at home with the family. I am a minister not just when I am leading a Bible study but also in the workplace. We are Christians not only on Sundays or when we are participating in church

123

activities. We are Christians all the time, so we must serve people in the name of Jesus Christ whenever and wherever we have the opportunity to do.

In order to live balanced lives, however, we must first be headed in the right direction. An airplane flying east from New York will never arrive in Seattle, no matter how well it is maintained or how expertly it is flown. The right direction spiritually is to view our work, indeed all of life, from an eternal perspective. Jesus said, "Do not store up for yourselves treasures on earth, where moth and rust destroy, and where thieves break in and steal. But store up for yourselves treasures in heaven, where moth and rust do not destroy, and where thieves do not break in and steal. For where your treasure is, there your heart will be also" (Matt. 6:19–21). "Do not work for food that spoils, but for food that endures to eternal life, which the Son of Man will give you" (John 6:27).

We must steward that which is temporal and give our lives to that which is eternal. Walter Henrichsen puts it this way: "Life is too short and the stakes too high for you to invest with 'wood, hay, and straw.' God gave you your days upon earth to prepare for an eternity with Him. What you build with your life appreciably influences the quality of your eternity with God"[1] (1 Cor. 3:11–15).

The Bible speaks about two things that endure forever: the Word of God and people. "Heaven and earth will pass away, but my words will never pass away" (Matt. 24:35). "For the perishable must clothe itself with the imperishable, and the mortal with immortality" (1Cor.15:53). Anything of eternal value will in some way relate to these two things. Our task as ministers of the Gospel is to bring the Word of God to bear upon the lives of people, knowing that the outcome of our ministry will have eternal consequences. "The words I have spoken to you are spirit and they are life" (John 6:63).

How do we invest in eternity? What can we do to lay up treasure in heaven? We must begin with a disciplined life of prayer and the study of God's Word, growing in our relationship with Christ, and living in obedience to God. We invest in eternity anytime we help people come to know Christ or grow in their relationship with Him. We lay up treasure in heaven anytime we serve people in His name. "And if anyone gives even a cup of cold water to one of these little ones because he is my disciple, I tell you the truth, he will certainly not lose his reward" (Matt. 10:42). Jesus commended those who fed the hungry, gave water to the thirsty, took strangers in, clothed the naked, and visited the sick and imprisoned. No act of kindness in His name will go unrewarded. "Always give yourselves fully to the work of the Lord, because you know that your labor in the Lord is not in vain" (1Cor. 15:58).

Missionaries are evaluated periodically by the organizations that sponsor them to ensure that they remain qualified and capable of continuing in that service. As missionaries in the marketplace, we too should periodically look at how effectively we are carrying out that assignment. Because of the distractions and demands of the workplace, plus Satan's efforts to hinder us, it is possible that our commitment to ministering in the workplace could fade. Therefore we must sometimes reevaluate ourselves by asking the following questions:

1. How effectively am I representing Jesus Christ in the workplace?
2. Do people around me know that I am a Christian?
3. To the best of my ability, am I living an obedient Christian life?
4. Am I on the lookout for opportunities to serve people?
5. Do I reach out to those who come my way?
6. Am I open to new and more effective ways to minister to people?"

At the same time, we should assess our job performance with such questions as these:

1. Am I experiencing contentment and fulfillment in my job?
2. Am I working as unto the Lord?
3. Am I the best employee I can be?

This is in keeping with these words of the apostle Paul to the Colossian church: "Whatever you do, work at it with all your heart, as working for the Lord, not for men, since you know that you will receive an inheritance from the Lord as a reward. It is the Lord Christ you are serving" (Col. 3:23–24).

What about retirement? Most people look forward to the time when they can give up their jobs and still receive a paycheck for the rest of their lives. Yet the Bible says nothing about retirement. It is true that the physical demands of some types of work necessitate retirement, yet there are many ways to be involved in meaningful and productive work. It is not uncommon today for a retiree to have a second or even a third career, having discovered soon after retirement the wisdom of God's plan for us to be meaningfully occupied.

After retirement, we should have more time, not less, for Christian service. Although the particular way in which we minister may change, we must continue in God's plan as long as we live. Some people find that their best and most productive years of ministry are the years when most have retired. This may be just what God intends. "The righteous will flourish like a palm tree, they will grow like a cedar of Lebanon; planted in the house of the LORD, they will flourish in the courts of our God. They will still bear fruit in old age, they will stay fresh and green, proclaiming, 'The LORD is upright; he is my Rock'" (Psalm 92:12–15).

NOTES

Chapter 1
1   J. Allan Petersen, *For Men Only* (Wheaton, IL: Tyndale House, 1981), 224.

Chapter 2
1   The words *ministry* and *minister* are derived from the Greek *diakonia, diakonos,* and *diakoneo,*which can also be translated "service," "servant," "attendant," and "deacon," along with their corresponding verbs.
2   Redemption is a term used to include both the ideas of deliverance and the price of that deliverance. To redeem is to buy back. God bought back sinners at the cost of His Son, Jesus Christ.
3   For the foregoing discussion of the priesthood, the author is indebted, in part, to Walter A. Henrichsen and William N. Garrison, *Layman, Look Up* (Grand Rapids: Zondervan Publishing House, 1983).

Chapter 3
1   Christopher Adsit, *Personal Disciplemaking* (Orlando, FL: Campus Crusade for Christ, 1996), 347.
2   Betty Lee Skinner, *Daws* (Grand Rapids; Zondervan, 1974), 39–40.

Chapter 4
1   Walter Henrichsen, *Thoughts from the Diary of a Desperate Man* (El Cajon, CA: Leadership Foundation, 1999), 34.
2   Source unknown.

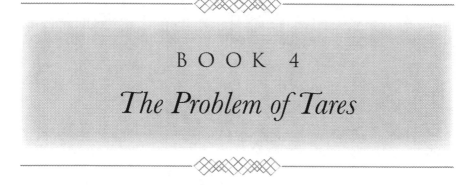

BOOK 4

The Problem of Tares

CONTENTS

"The kingdom of heaven may be compared to a man who sowed good seed in his field. But while his men were sleeping, his enemy came and sowed tares among the wheat and went away."
—Matthew 13:24–25

PARABLE OF THE WHEAT AND THE TARES *

Matthew 13:24–30, 36–43

Jesus told them another parable:

"The kingdom of heaven is like a man who sowed good seed in his field. But while everyone was sleeping, his enemy came and sowed weeds among the wheat, and went away. When the wheat sprouted and formed heads, then the weeds also appeared.

"The owner's servants came to him and said, 'Sir, didn't you sow good seed in your field? Where then did the weeds come from?'

"'An enemy did this,' he replied.

"The servants asked him, 'Do you want us to go and pull them up?'

"'No,' he answered, 'because while you are pulling the weeds, you may root up the wheat with them. Let both grow together until the harvest. At that time I will tell the harvesters: First collect the weeds and tie them in bundles to be burned; then gather the wheat and bring it into my barn.'"

Then he left the crowd and went into the house.

His disciples came to him and said, "Explain to us the parable of the weeds in the field.

He answered, "The one who sowed the good seed is the Son of Man. The field is the world, and the good seed stands for the sons of the kingdom. The weeds are the sons of the evil one, and the enemy who sows them is the devil. The harvest is the end of the age, and the harvesters are angels.

"As the weeds are pulled up and burned in the fire, so it will be at the end of the age. The Son of Man will send out his angels, and they will weed out of his kingdom everything that causes sin and all who do evil. They will throw them into the fiery furnace, where there will be weeping and gnashing of teeth. Then the righteous will shine like the sun in the kingdom of their Father. He who has ears, let him hear.

*Tares: the bearded darnel, mentioned only in Matthew 13:25–30. It is the Lolium temulentum, a species of ryegrass, the seeds of which are a strong soporific poison. It bears the closest resemblance to wheat till the ear appears, and only then the difference is discovered. It grows plentifully in Syria and Palestine. (From Easton's Bible Dictionary, PC Study Bible formatted electronic database, copyright © 2003 Biblesoft, Inc.)

INTRODUCTION

Satan plants counterfeit Christians in churches and, as with the tares and wheat, it is often impossible to distinguish them from the genuine. People are added to church rolls through false, though sincere, professions of faith, while many who have attended church from childhood grow up without ever being saved. They attend services and participate in religious activities, yet they never come to know Christ as Savior and Lord.

John Stott addresses this in *Basic Christianity*:

> We have also to recognize that not all members of the visible church are necessarily members of the real church of Jesus Christ. Some whose names are inscribed on the church rolls and registers have never had their names, as Jesus put it, "written in heaven." Although this is a fact to which the Bible often refers, yet it is not for us to judge: "the Lord knows those who are His." The minister by baptism welcomes into the visible church those who profess faith in Christ. But only God knows those who actually exercise faith, for only God sees in the heart. No doubt the two largely overlap, but they are not identical.[1]

The church[2] is in trouble. Most of the work is done by relatively few of the people. Many church members never attend services on a regular basis or read and study the Bible. There may be more than ever widespread apathy, indifference, and unconcern for winning people to Jesus Christ. Pastors and other ministers are unable to motivate and mobilize people for effective ministry, the result being that churches often fail to impact their communities with the Gospel. Outsiders rarely visit churches because of the hypocrisy they see in the lives of some who profess to be Christians.

Consequently, the body of Christ suffers, the witness of Christ is impaired, and the work of Christ is severely hindered.

But the greatest tragedy of all is that countless church members go through life with the mistaken notion that they are saved, when all the while they are still walking in the darkness of sin. Arthur W. Pink, in *Exposition of the Sermon on the Mount*, says this:

> Never were there so many millions of nominal Christians on earth as there are today, and never was there such a small percentage of real ones. Not since before the days of Luther and Calvin, when the great Reformation effected such a great change for the better, has Christendom been so crowded with those who have "a form of godliness" but who are strangers of its transforming power. We seriously doubt whether there has ever been a time in the history of this Christian era when there were such multitudes of deceived souls within the churches, who verily believe that all is well with their souls when in fact the wrath abides on them.[3]

The problem of tares could not be stated more clearly.

The following is a look at five critical mistakes
committed by churches today
that Satan employs in sowing tares among the wheat.

CHAPTER 1

SUGARCOATING THE GOSPEL

"I did not shrink from declaring to you anything that was profitable, and teaching you publicly and from house to house, solemnly testifying to both Jews and Greeks of repentance toward God and faith in our Lord Jesus Christ."

—Acts 20:20–21

Salvation can be neither earned nor inherited. It cannot be obtained through religious rituals or ordinances, nor can it be bestowed by the church or acquired through any human endeavor or man-made institution. Salvation involves God's grace and man's faith. Grace is God's unmerited favor toward man, while faith is man's response to grace. The Bible says, "Believe in the Lord Jesus, and you will be saved, you and your household" (Acts 16:31) and "For God so loved the world, that He gave His only begotten Son, that whoever believes in Him shall not perish, but have eternal life" (John 3:16). Faith has both an inward and an outward dimension—inward trust and outward confession, as the following passage makes clear:

> But what does it say? "The Word is in you, in your mouth and in your heart"—that is, the word of faith which we are preaching, that if you confess with your mouth Jesus as Lord, and believe in your heart that God raised Him from the dead, you will be saved; for with the heart a person believes, resulting in righteousness, and with the mouth he confesses, resulting in salvation. (Rom. 10:8–10)

There may be no better illustration of the meaning of *saving faith* than that of a parachute. When a man jumps out of an airplane with nothing but his parachute between himself and eternity, he is putting his faith to the highest test. Until he exits the plane, however, his claim to believe in the parachute is meaningless. In the same way, to be saved, a person must commit himself totally to Jesus Christ. It is not enough to merely say that he is a believer—he must obey the Gospel. This requires more than just an individual belief that Jesus is the Son of God and Savior of the world. His claim must be backed up by total surrender, an absolute yielding of his life to Christ.

But the Bible also says, "I tell you, no, but unless you repent, you will all likewise perish" (Luke 13:3) and "The Lord is not slow about His promise, as some count slowness, but is patient toward you, not wishing for any to perish but for all to come to repentance" (2 Peter 3:9). To repent is to change one's mind or attitude about sin—to forsake sin and turn toward God. A proper view of salvation requires at least some understanding of both repentance and faith, for they are inseparably bound.

John Stott writes,

> Let me be more explicit about the forsaking which cannot be separated from the following of Jesus Christ. First there must be a renunciation of sin. This, in a word, is repentance. It is the first part of Christian conversion. It can in no circumstances be bypassed. Repentance and faith belong together. We cannot follow Christ without forsaking sin. Repentance is a definite turn from every thought, word, deed, and habit which is known to be wrong. It is not sufficient to feel pangs of remorse or to make some kind of apology to God. Fundamentally, repentance is a matter neither of emotion nor of speech. It is an inward change of mind and attitude towards sin which leads to a change of behavior.[1]

The apostle John uses *confession*, a word close in meaning to *repentance*. "If we confess our sins, He is faithful and righteous to forgive us our sins and to cleanse us from all unrighteousness" (1 John 1:9). To confess is to agree with God about our sins—to see our sins as He sees them. Confession always precedes forgiveness. To preach faith without repentance is not biblical preaching and will not lead to forgiveness and to the conversion of sinners. Preachers must confront their listeners not only with the fact of sin but also with its eternal consequences and the need to forsake it. Evangelist Billy Graham would conclude his evangelistic services with this appeal to his hearers: "You must repent and you must receive Christ." An invitation to follow Christ must begin where He began: "Repent, and believe in the gospel" (Mark 1:15).

Regrettably, all too often, this is not done. In many churches, repentance is an unfamiliar word because it is never preached. Instead, it has given way to another gospel—a sugarcoated, watered-down gospel that says, "Just ask Jesus into your heart." I would suggest that such an invitation is foreign to the New Testament, with the possible exception of Revelation 3:20: "Behold, I stand at the door and knock; if anyone hears My voice and opens the door, I will come in to him and will dine with him, and he with Me." Note, however, that this invitation is not to lost sinners who need to be saved, but to the lukewarm, indifferent church at Laodicea, and that even here it is coupled with a command to repent: "Therefore be zealous and repent" (Rev. 3:19). There is just no escaping the necessity of repentance.

Preachers must not be afraid to proclaim the hard truth that that those who do not repent will perish—that they will experience conscious suffering in a godless eternity. Without the message that "Jesus loves me this I know, for the Bible tells me so," we must return to the preaching of earlier eras when such sermons as "Sinners in the Hands of an Angry God" and "Pay Day Someday" would not have been uncommon. The appeal "Give your heart to Jesus" must include the exhortation, "Repent, then, and turn to God, so that your sins may be wiped out" (Acts 3:19 NIV).

Bold proclamation of truth was at the center and at the heart of worship in the early church, and with phenomenal results. The apostles preached not for enjoyment or entertainment but for conviction, and as a result, the church grew in a manner that has never been surpassed. As the Bible says, "So then, those who had received his word were baptized; and that day there were added about three thousand souls. They were continually devoting themselves to the apostles' teaching and to fellowship, to the breaking of bread and to prayer" (Acts 2:41–42).

Where in the Bible does it say, "Just give your heart to Jesus," or "Pray this prayer, and you will be saved"? Granted, such an appeal may bring to Christ one whom the Holy Spirit has prepared, but it may do a grave injustice to others by not confronting them with their sins. Instead of telling people to "pray this prayer, and you will be saved," ministers must make them understand that "having overlooked the times of ignorance, God is now declaring to men that all people everywhere should repent, because He has fixed a day in which He will judge the world in righteousness through a Man whom He has appointed, having furnished proof to all men by raising Him from the dead" (Acts 17:30–31).

Why this missing emphasis on repentance? Is it because preachers are afraid they will offend their congregations by preaching a hard gospel? The apostle Paul wrote, "For am I now seeking the favor of men, or of God? Or am I striving to please men? If I were still trying to please men, I would not be a bond-servant of Christ" (Gal.1:10).

How many deceived souls have responded to an invitation to "accept Christ," only to remain alienated from the Savior for lack of repentance? The cleansing power of the blood of Jesus Christ is ineffectual for the unrepentant sinner. "He who conceals his transgressions will not prosper, but he who confesses and forsakes them will find compassion" (Prov. 28:13). Church rolls swell with the addition of those who unknowingly make false professions of faith, but the church is weakened as these tares crowd the wheat. They may be attracted to the fellowship of believers, but for one reason or another, they continue in the manner of the unconverted, bearing no spiritual fruit in their lives and helping to produce none in the lives of others.

A sugarcoated, watered-down Gospel is not the message of the Bible. Anything less than "repent and believe in the Gospel" is not biblical preaching and must be avoided, for it does irreparable harm to the church and brings eternal ruin to many.

CHAPTER 2

ABANDONING THE NEWBORN*

"Like newborn babies, long for the pure milk of the word,
so that by it you may grow in respect to salvation."
—1 Peter 2:2

The needs of a new Christian are much like those of a newborn baby:
love, food, and protection. After assurance of salvation, he needs love and
acceptance by the body of Christ. He must be fed spiritually and taught
how to feed himself from the Word of God. He must be protected from
whatever would harm him but especially from Satan's efforts to neutralize
his faith and hinder his spiritual growth. Pastors and evangelists agree
that the fruits of evangelism must be conserved. Those wanting to follow
Christ must not be allowed to come to the threshold of the kingdom of God
and then be lost for lack of proper nourishment. No ministry should be
more important to the life of a church than that of following-up decisions
to accept Christ. Whether it is done through an organized program or
through a personal ministry of a few dedicated laymen, it must be given
top priority.

Christopher B. Adsit, in *Personal Disciple-Making*, says this:

> After water baptism, the newly identified believer needs
> the church members to do a lot more than just shake
> his hand, slap him on the back and say, "Live long and
> prosper," and then leave him to fend for himself. They
> now have the responsibility of bringing him into their

local body for the purpose of protection, instruction and ministry.[1]

We sometimes hear about a baby dying for lack of care. This is not only tragic—it is criminal. Who would bring an infant into the world and fail to provide it with nourishment and care? Yet churches often abandon their newborn, and nobody seems to care. This is most unfortunate, for these new converts then run the risk of remaining spiritual infants for the rest of their lives, or worse still, of dying. Evangelist Billy Graham said, "Decision is five percent, following through on the decision is ninety-five percent."

Paul wrote to the church at Corinth, "And I, brethren, could not speak to you as to spiritual men, but as to men of flesh, as to infants in Christ. I gave you milk to drink, not solid food; for you were not yet able to receive it. Indeed, even now you are not yet able" (1 Cor. 3:1–2). Without follow-up, new Christians will remain babes and will not mature spiritually. Even worse, those whose decisions are sincere but who lack genuine saving faith may lose the opportunity to become true believers.

On the other hand, those whose decisions are not genuine but who are engaged in an effective follow-up ministry may well come to know the Savior through the process. For this reason, young children can make a profession of faith that, real or not at the time, may eventually bear fruit as long as they are brought up in a Christ-centered home, where the process of follow-up and disciple-making can occur naturally.

Many churches have a thought process something like this: "The pastor and staff are too busy to spend time with new converts. We will enroll them in Sunday school and have someone visit them with information about the activities and programs of the church. Involving them in the life of the church will ensure their spiritual well-being, especially if people are praying for them. Those who have grown up in the church will not need much help anyway."

Compare this with the words of Paul to the Thessalonians: "But we proved to be gentle among you, as a nursing mother tenderly cares for her own children. Having so fond an affection for you, we were well-pleased to impart to you not only the gospel of God but also our own lives, because you had become very dear to us" (1 Thess. 2:7–8).

Paul and his coworkers were willing to impart their own lives to ensure the well-being of their spiritual offspring, yet the attitude in many churches is that enrolling new converts in Sunday school is the only thing necessary for their spiritual survival and growth. Sunday school may be vital to a healthy church, but it cannot replace a ministry tailored to meet the immediate needs of a new believer. (Author's note: I have been teaching Sunday school for more than forty years.)

As an example of what can be done in this area, I know a layman, an experienced disciple-maker who volunteered to lead a follow-up ministry for new converts in his church. He would contact them the same day that they made their public decisions for Christ, provide them with some follow-up literature, and arrange to attend a special class for new believers. For five consecutive weeks, during the Sunday school hour, he would instruct these new believers in the fundamentals of the faith, after which they were directed to an appropriate Sunday school class. The sessions would be repeated every five weeks, allowing new converts to join at any time for their period of instruction.

Tragically, the primary concern of some is to obtain *decisions* for the church's annual report. It is sad, indeed, when the *ministry* becomes more important than the souls who are the object of the ministry—when the *number* of people baptized takes precedence over the spiritual well-being of the people. No minister would ever admit this, perhaps even to himself, but his actions speak loudly and clearly.

Jesus said, "What man among you, if he has a hundred sheep and has lost one of them, does not leave the ninety-nine in the open pasture and go after the one which is lost until he finds it?" (Luke 15:4). Many churches today seem content to let not just the one but the ninety-nine wander off if much effort is required to keep and protect them. As long as decisions for Christ are seen as statistics rather than as people seeking salvation, there will be very little incentive for follow-up. God forbid that the leaders of any church who confesses Jesus Christ as Lord would lack either the ability or the willingness to provide the nurturing necessary to establish new believers in the faith.

A busy pastor may know that he must get around to implementing "that all-important follow-up program for new Christians," but it always seems to get edged out by other programs and activities. It may be that he just cannot find anyone to work in this area of ministry. As a result, new believers often receive woefully inadequate nurturing, or else they are simply abandoned altogether.

Thus one aspect of Satan's strategy for sowing tares among the wheat is to ensure that those who want to follow Christ are never given the opportunity tocome alive spiritually. If he can keep them out of the Word of God, and the Word out of them, he can stop the growth process before it ever begins. It is the Word that gives life, and Satan knows it.

*Some of the contents of this chapter appear also in sections 2 and 3 of book 1, *Disciple/Disciple-Maker.*

CHAPTER 3

LOSING SIGHT OF LORDSHIP

Then Jesus said to His disciples, "If anyone wishes to come after Me, he must deny himself, and take up his cross and follow Me."

—Matthew 16:24

For many, being a Christian is like the teenage boy who wants all he can get from his father but refuses to accept and yield to parental authority. He wants to drive the family car on Friday and Saturday nights but chooses not to obey the midnight curfew imposed by his father. He enjoys the comfort of a nice home but rebels when told to clean his room and take out the trash. He expects a weekly allowance but ignores his father's advice about how to use it.

Robert Shank, in *Life in the Son*, writes,

> One cannot accept Christ and His salvation on lesser terms than the complete surrender of self to Him. We pastors have confused the issue by such pulpit appeals as, "You have accepted Christ as your Savior, but have you really made Him the Lord of your life? Why not dedicate your life fully to Him?" Such appeals imply that acceptance of Christ as Savior and as Lord are two entirely separate acts. Much to the contrary, they are inseparable aspects of a single act. Like repentance and faith, they are mutually involved; there cannot be one without the other. No man can accept Jesus as the Savior of his soul without accepting

Him as Lord of his life. Multitudes of "Christians" today
seem quite unaware of this solemn fact.[1]

Many want the security of God's salvation but rebel against His
rule in their lives. They do not understand what it means to obey the
Gospel. "Lordship" is not in their vocabulary. In *True Discipleship*, William
MacDonald says, "True Christianity is an all-out commitment to the Lord
Jesus Christ. The Savior is not looking for man and women who will give
Him their spare evenings, their weekends, or their years of retirement.
Rather He seeks those who will give Him first place in their lives."[2]

John Stott says it this way:

> The astonishing idea is current in some circles that
> we can enjoy the benefits of Christ's salvation without
> accepting the challenge of His sovereign lordship. Such
> an unbalanced notion is not to be found in the New
> Testament. "Jesus is Lord" is the earliest known creed
> of Christians. In days when imperial Rome was pressing
> its citizens to say "Caesar is Lord," these words had a
> dangerous flavor. But Christians did not flinch. They
> could not give Caesar their first allegiance, because they
> had already given it to Imperial Jesus.[3]

The Christian life is a life of obedience to Jesus Christ. Anything less
than absolute surrender to the Lordship of Christ and unswerving devotion
to His Word falls short of God's plan for those who would be a disciple
of Christ. It is essential, therefore, that the church understand, practice,
and exhort every believer in the terms of discipleship laid out by the Lord
Jesus Christ. Where the church has lost sight of lordship and failed to
emphasize obedience in conjunction with salvation, it has paid dearly, for
what remains are weak congregations made up largely of immature and
spiritually unproductive members.

According to MacDonald,

> The Lord made stringent demands on those who would be
> His disciples—demands that are all but overlooked in this
> day of luxury living. Too often we look upon Christianity
> as an escape from hell and a guarantee of heaven. Beyond

that, we feel that we have every right to enjoy the best that this life has to offer. We know that there are strong verses on discipleship in the Bible, but we have difficulty reconciling them with our ideas of what Christianity should be. [4]

But how does this relate to the problem of tares, since tares represent unsaved people in the church? Consider what happens when church leaders separate salvation from lordship in their preaching and teaching: those who would follow Christ, ignorant of the true meaning of discipleship, embark upon so-called Christian lives that are destined to failure. Theirs is an easy, inauthentic Christianity, an imitation of the real thing. Where obedience to God's Word is not emphasized, most Christians stand little chance of true lordship, and as a result, they grow very little and bear little to no spiritual fruit. These people become comfortable in a church that never challenges them to an all-out surrender of their lives to Christ. As for those whose lives were never marked by genuine repentance and faith, and seeds of life remaining in them that might have germinated never have the opportunity to do so. Tragically, they remain tares in the church, and as their numbers increase, that church becomes a lifeless mausoleum.

The New Testament also expresses obedience as "good works," and while good works contribute nothing toward our salvation, they are nevertheless the natural result of union with Christ: "For by grace you have been saved through faith; and that not of yourselves, it is the gift of God; not as a result of works, so that no one may boast. For we are His workmanship, created in Christ Jesus for good works, which God prepared beforehand so that we would walk in them" (Eph. 2:8–10). A life of good works is the mark of a genuine Christian, while the absence of such works may call into question the validity of a person's profession.

Dietrich Bonhoeffer writes about faith and obedience in *The Cost of Discipleship*: "Faith is only real when there is obedience, never without it, and faith only becomes faith in the act of obedience."[5] Preachers must communicate to their congregations this biblical mandate for true believers to continue in unswerving obedience to the Lord Jesus Christ. This is the meaning of lordship. Those who fail to do this jeopardize the eternal well-being of those in the church who are not saved and thereby add to the problem of tares. Such people can wind up in either heaven or hell, depending upon their understanding, or misunderstanding, of the command not only to *believe* but to *obey* the Gospel.

CHAPTER 4

AT EASE IN ZION

"But the one who endures to the end, he will be saved."
—Mark 13:13

Perhaps no biblical doctrine has generated more debate than that concerning the security of the believer—whether a person who has been genuinely saved can abandon his faith in Christ and be lost once again. One reason for this is that there is so much scripture from which advocates of either position can argue their case. My purpose here is to point out how this issue relates to the problem of tares. It seems that we rarely hear sermons based upon the following passages of scripture:

> For in the case of those who have once been enlightened and have tasted of the heavenly gift and have been made partakers of the Holy Spirit, and have tasted the good word of God and the powers of the age to come, and then have fallen away, it is impossible to renew them again to repentance, since they again crucify to themselves the Son of God and put Him to open shame. (Heb. 6:4–6)

> Behold I, Paul, say to you that if you receive circumcision, Christ will be of no benefit to you. And I testify again to every man who receives circumcision, that he is under obligation to keep the whole Law. You have been severed from Christ, you who are seeking to be justified by law; you have fallen from grace. (Gal. 5:2–4)

Some view these as contradictory to the doctrine of "unconditional security of the believer."[1] Preachers often make it a point to avoid scripture passages that do not easily conform to their particular theology. They choose to avoid them rather than face their congregations with hard biblical truths that they, themselves, may not fully grasp.

As for the many warning passages found in the New Testament, to disregard them is to ignore one of the most important truths in scripture—Christ's command to persevere to the end.[2] Where there is no warning against falling away, there will be no serious exhortation to keep going; where perseverance is not preached, it may not be practiced, especially by those who are immature in the faith.

If there is no need for perseverance, why did Jesus say, "Those who endure to the end will be saved" (Matt. 24:13)? What then becomes of those who do not endure (persevere) to the end? Were they genuine believers in the beginning? Some say no, because true believers will always persevere to the end. Others say a person cannot continue what he has never begun—in this case, a life of obedience to Christ, so He must have been speaking only about true believers. Regardless of what we may believe about the security of the believer and the possibility of apostasy (falling away), these warning passages are in the Bible for a purpose. To ignore them is to do so at our own peril.

But preachers do not need to renounce their belief in unconditional security of the believer in order to teach and preach from the warning passages of the Bible. Indeed, for many Christians, the exhortations found in these passages may be the key to their persevering, while for the unsaved, they may God's way of bringing them to saving faith. Would that every preacher of the Gospel could say, like Paul, "For I did not shrink from declaring to you the whole purpose of God" (Acts 20:27).

As a young lieutenant, I spent eight backbreaking weeks undergoing ranger training at the US Army Infantry School. This course was designed to test our physical and psychological limits, train us in small group leadership skills, and prepare us for service in Vietnam. Whether we were at the ranger camp at Fort Benning, Georgia, the mountains of north Georgia, or the swamps of the Florida panhandle, we were constantly aware that the key to completion of the course was unceasing perseverance. The coveted ranger patch would be awarded only to those who endured to the end.

How much more important it is to persevere in the Christian life! Every worldly achievement will vanish when compared to the heavenly reward for obedience to Jesus Christ. Paul wrote to Timothy, "I have fought the good fight, I have finished the course, I have kept the faith; in the future there is laid up for me the crown of righteousness, which the Lord, the righteous Judge, will award to me on that day; and not only to me, but also to all who have loved His appearing" (2 Tim. 4:7–8).

Edward Charles Dagan writes,

> Men sometimes make the mistake of taking this initial act of repentance and faith as if that completed all that man had to do in order to be saved; and in a sense, that is true, provided that faith and repentance be continued. But the Scriptures show that there must be this continuance, and this is what we call perseverance.[3]

Robert Shank expresses it well:

> There is no warrant for that strange at-ease-in-Zion definition of perseverance which assures Christians that perseverance is inevitable and relieves them of the necessity of deliberately persevering in faith, encouraging them to place confidence in some past act or experience. Many, quite uncommonly, have transferred their faith from Christ Himself to the fact of a past conversion experience and the assumed validity of the popular doctrine on "once in grace, always in grace." Their confidence now rests, not actually in Christ Himself, but in their conversion experience sometime in the past. They know the time and place they made a decision; but they do not know Christ. They have no sense of present need for Him—no sense of present dependence on Christ for saving grace, no living faith in a living Savior. They are tares among the wheat—tares in the church.[4]

Dale Moody makes this significant observation:

> Warnings against the danger of falling away from the faith may be noted in every New Testament writing

but Philemon, which has no doctrinal discussion at all. Why then has this teaching been excluded in much of the Christian theology of the West? The answer on examination comes home loud and clear: tradition has triumphed over Scripture.[5]

The effect that this error of ignoring warning passages has had on the church is indeed grievous. Only God knows how many people have been lost to His eternal kingdom because they failed to persevere in their faith. A person is in jeopardy when he can say, "Since I am saved, I can live as I please. Though I sometimes sin and backslide, it will be okay for me in the end."

Finally, if preachers would preach and teach the warning passages of the Bible, along with the need for perseverance in the faith, with the same passion with which they proclaim salvation apart from works, the church would find its members persevering in their Christian lives as never before. New converts and older Christians alike would remain faithful and spiritually productive in the life of the church. No longer would a large segment of the average congregation be useless to the cause of Christ—tares among the wheat—and in danger of God's eternal judgment because of a theology that denies the possibility of falling away.[6]

CHAPTER 5

BUSY HERE AND THERE

"A man turned aside and brought a man to me and said, 'Guard this man; if for any reason he is missing, then your life shall be for his life, or else you shall pay a talent of silver.' While your servant was busy here and there, he was gone."

—1 Kings 20:39–40

Eternity will reveal how many are gone forever because the church was "busy here and here." They may not be gone physically; they attend church regularly, but they are gone spiritually because they do not know Christ. Dawson Trotman refers to the busyness of the church as "the curse of today, busy doing Christian things—spiritual activity with little productivity."[1] Howard Hendricks says that "much of the feverish and frustrating activity of the contemporary church is devoid of relevance and fulfillment. Entertainment, not education, is our program."[2] This fruitless activity is responsible for its share of tares in the church today.

The twofold task of the church is (1) to reach the lost with the Gospel of Jesus Christ,

> Go therefore and make disciples of all the nations, baptizing them in the name of the Father and the Son and the Holy Spirit, teaching them to observe all that I commanded you; and lo, I am with you always, even to the end of the age (Matt. 28:19–20);

and (2) to edify or build up believers:

> And He gave some as apostles, and some as prophets, and some as evangelists, and some as pastors and teachers, for the equipping of the saints for the work of service, to the building up of the body of Christ; until we all attain to the unity of the faith, and of the knowledge of the Son of God, to a mature man, to the measure of the stature which belongs to the fullness of Christ. (Eph. 4:11–13)

All activity in the church must be evaluated in light of these biblical mandates. Stated another way, it must be redemptive.[3]

Some activities are inherently redemptive: worship services, Bible studies, prayer meetings, mission work, ministry training, and evangelism. (But even these can fail to function in a redemptive manner, such as a worship service in which the Gospel is distorted.)Other activities are redemptive only if they are made to be so: health and fitness, sports, arts and crafts, drama, and church outing and trips.

This is not to say that most church programs and activities do not in some way contribute to the edifying of the body or the evangelization of the lost—only that they are but lifeless activities if they do not do so. Unfortunately, church priorities are often shifted in favor of things that are the least productive from an eternal perspective. The result is that church members often confuse Christian activity with productivity, and fewer unsaved members come into a saving knowledge of Christ.

I once volunteered to lead an evangelistic outreach program in an effort to increase Sunday school attendance. We began with ten people participating in the weekly home visits, but as the weeks passed, the number dwindled to three—the pastor, the youth director, and myself. Soon, they, too, got busy with other activities, and the program collapsed, though nobody seemed to notice. When church leaders mistake Christian activity for fruitful, redemptive ministry, what can be expected of new converts and others still weak in their faith? Many will not know the difference between meaningful, life-changing ministry and activities that offer little in the way of spiritual growth and development. It is altogether possible for unsaved people to be swept up in the busy life of an energetic church and never come face-to-face with matters of repentance, faith, and the need for forgiveness of sins.

But the same can be said for traditional church structures and activities, as in the case of worship services that become dominated by Christian entertainment, or Sunday school classes where meaningful Bible teaching is allocated to whatever time remains after socializing, announcements, activity planning, and lengthy prayer sessions.

Howard Snyder addresses this in *The Community of the King*:

> Church structure must be biblically valid. How devoted we become to preserving programs and how little devoted we are to each other or to structures that help us truly be the Church. We need to ask some hard (and to some people, shocking) questions. Is the traditional Sunday school structure truly defensible? Do believers really worship or encounter God in our church services? Is the Word of God really taught and heard? Do believers really "speak the truth in love" to one another, or only say nice, meaningless things?
>
> Quite simply, the criterion of biblical validity means that all church structures should in fact help the Church be the Church and carry out its mission. They should be structures which promote community, build disciples, and sustain witness. Structures which in fact do this are valid; structures which do not are invalid, regardless of how esthetic, efficient, or venerated they may be.[4]

One thing that sets the church apart from service clubs and community groups is that it is not just an organization but a living organism whose mission is redemptive. I once belonged to a civic club in the small town where we lived. The club met once a week for lunch, business, and a program. I enjoyed the meetings, the programs, and the camaraderie and felt good about the worthwhile community service the club performed. But it did not compare to the church with its weekly worship services, the preaching and teaching of the Bible, the fellowship of believers, and various ministry opportunities. We must be careful not to let the church become a Sunday-morning club!

In *Disciples Are Made—Not Born*, Walter Henrichsen writes the following about the redemptive function of the church:

I once had the privilege of observing church in upper Michigan. Every year, the pastor, along with the elders, would ask the representatives from each group in the church to defend their right for existence on the basis of two criteria: (1) The legitimacy of their goals and objectives; and (2) the degree to which they achieved these goal and objectives. If any group did not meet both of these criteria, the elders of the church would disband it. What a terrific idea! If we would ruthlessly apply this practice in all of our churches, it would doubtless contribute to a more vital and healthy fellowship.[5]

Jesus warned the religious leaders with these words: "Woe to you, scribes and Pharisees, hypocrites! For you tithe mint and dill and cummin, and have neglected the weightier provisions of the law: justice and mercy and faithfulness; but these are the things you should have done without neglecting the others" (Matt. 23:23). The church must not be satisfied with doing things that are good in place of things that are essential. While we should not neglect legitimate things of lesser importance, we must never lose sight of the weightier matters—winning to Christ those who are lost and building up the church. We must be careful about being busy here and there, for in so doing, we may deprive many of a genuine experience with Christ and make worse the problem of tares.

NOTES

Parable

1   *The New Unger's Bible Dictionary.* Originally published by Moody Press of Chicago, Illinois. Copyright (c) 1988.

Introduction

1   John Stott, *Basic Christianity* (Downers Grove, IL: Inter-Varsity Press, 1958), 104– 105.

2   Unless otherwise indicated, the word *church* is used in this book to mean the local congregation or, in a general sense, to all churches, as opposed to the universal church or worldwide body of believers, in which case it is capitalized. When the church is said to do, act, think, or carry out any other human function, it refers to the collective body of church members, the ministers and leaders of the local church, or any others in the church who are responsible for ministry.

3   Arthur W. Pink, *An Exposition of the Sermon on the Mount* (Grand Rapids, MI: Baker Book House,1950), 377.

Chapter 1

1   John Stott, *Basic Christianity*, 109–110.

Chapter 2

1   Christopher Adsit, *Personal Disciple-Making* (Orlando, FL: Campus Crusade for Christ, 1996), 43.

Chapter 3

1   Robert Shank, *Life in the Son* (Springfield, MO: Westcott, 1960), 15.

2   William MacDonald, *True Discipleship* (Kansas City, KS: Walterick Publishers, 1975), 5.

3   John Stott, *Basic Christianity*, 112.

4   William MacDonald, *True Discipleship*, 5.

5   Dietrich Bonhoeffer, *The Cost of Discipleship* (New York, NY: Macmillan, 1949), 69.

Chapter 4

1   "Unconditional security of the believer" means that a person who has come to Christ in repentance and faith is forever secure in Christ. He can never again be lost as a result of any future sin or falling away from the faith.
2   The following are examples of New Testament passages cited by Shank as warning against falling away and/or exhorting to perseverance: Colossians 1:20–23; 1Timothy 1:18–20; 6:9–10; Hebrews 6:4–6; 10:26–31; 12:14–17, 25–29; James 5:19–20; 2 Peter 2:1–22; 1 John 5:16; Revelation 2:10–11.
3   Edward Charles Dagan, *The Doctrines of Our Faith* (Nashville, TN: The Sunday School Board of the Southern Baptist Convention), 134.
4   Robert Shank, *Life in the Son*, 264.
5   Dale Moody, *The Word of Truth* (Grand Rapids, MI: William B. Publishing Company, 1981), 358.
6   It should be noted that the author of this book affirms his personal belief in "the unconditional security of the believer."

Chapter 5

1   Dawson Trotman, *Born to Reproduce* (Colorado Springs, CO: Navpress, 1956), 24.
2   Walter Henrichsen, *Disciples Are Made—Not Born* (Wheaton, IL: Victor Books, 1975), 5.
3   The word *redemptive* is used in this chapter to mean ministry, the goal of which is to help people come to know Christ or in some way help them to grow toward maturity in Christ.
4   Howard A. Snyder, *Community of the King* (Downers Grove, IL: Inter-Varsity Press), 140–141.
5   Walter Henrichsen, *Disciples Are Made—Not Born*, 66.

BOOK 5
The Doctrine of Rewards

CONTENTS

"For the Son of Man is going to come in his Father's glory with his angels, and then he will reward each person according to what he has done."
—Matthew 16:27

CHAPTER 1

ETERNAL ACCOUNTABILITY

The message of the Gospel is that God has provided a way of redemption for the human race through His Son, Jesus Christ. This is the basis of our eternal hope. We who have trusted in Christ for salvation are saved by God's grace and will be transformed into the very likeness of Christ when He returns. We will spend eternity in heaven, the dwelling place of God, where even now Christ is interceding for us (Heb. 7:25).

Yet in the face of this glorious truth, there is a further consideration to which we must pay careful attention. It is quite clear from the scriptures that even for the Christian, there is to be a day of reckoning. The following words of the apostle Paul speak directly to both the present and future life of a Christian. "For we must all appear before the judgment seat of Christ, that each one may receive what is due him for the things done while in the body, whether good or bad" (2 Cor. 5:10). All believers, whether living or dead at Christ's coming, must face Him in judgment. "For we will all stand before God's judgment seat … So then, each of us will give an account of himself to God" (Rom. 14:10, 12). *Grace does not eliminate accountability*. There are eternal consequences for temporal behavior. Every child of God must therefore examine the conduct of his life in light of this profound biblical truth.

Accountability is the biblical principle that as free moral agents, entirely dependent upon God for our existence, we are answerable to Him for our thoughts, words, and deeds. Jesus spoke of accountability when He said, "From everyone who has been given much, much will be demanded; and from the one who has been entrusted with much, much more will be asked" (Luke 12:48). Without accountability, we are free to ignore the law. (Would we observe the speed limit if we knew that we would never be ticketed for violating it?) Similarly, if there was no eternal accountability for the way we live now, we could ignore the commands of God, for we would never have to answer to Him. But God's grace does not set aside the judgment that we will face when Christ returns. In this general expectation of judgment, many Christians are comfortable with the thought that they are safe. They should realize instead that "the time is come for judgment to begin at the house of God" (1 Peter 4:17).

It is important to note that in writing about the judgment seat of Christ, the apostle Paul is not suggesting the punishment of sin, as though there was something lacking in the justification already imputed to the believer. "Through him everyone who believes is justified from everything you could not be justified from by the Law of Moses" (Acts 13:39) and "There is now no condemnation for those who are in Christ Jesus" (Rom. 8:1). Nor is he proposing a doctrine of merit to accompany justification, as though the believer's ability to stand before Christ depends to some degree upon himself and not entirely upon the grace and mercy of God. To the contrary, Paul's meaning is clear in light of 1 Corinthians 3:10–15. This passage may be paraphrased as follows:

> Every believer is to build (live his life) upon the foundation which is Jesus Christ—a foundation upon which he is secure for all eternity. The Christian's work of building will be made clear on the day of Christ's judgment, tested and tried, as if by fire. Those things that remain will bring reward, while those things that do not survive will result in loss.

The judgment seat of Christ serves the purpose of absolute justice, vindicating both the holiness and the impartiality of God. It is a solemn reminder that the moral values of God's universe have not ceased, though the believer, under the grace of God, has been justified by faith and made secure in Christ for all eternity. It is indeed the Christian whose life should reflect the fruit of moral consistency: "Written not with ink but with the Spirit of the living God, not on tablets of stone but on tablets of human hearts" (2 Cor. 3:3). The impartiality of Christ's judgment may be noted in the assurance that each individual will receive reward or loss on the basis of his or her own life, whether good or bad. The purpose of this judgment is retribution. It is a paying back for what has or has not been done; it involves the disclosure not only of what has been worthless but also of what has been good and valuable in this life. The judgment is an assessment of worth, with the assignment of rewards to those who deserve them and the loss or withholding of rewards from those who do not deserve them.

The rewards themselves will likely vary in proportion to the faithfulness and diligence of the individual. We do not know all the implications and consequences of standing before the judgment seat of Christ, yet it is clear that the believer will be answerable for the quality of this present life. We can only speculate as to the nature of the rewards that are mentioned so often in the New Testament. (The word *reward* is found twenty-five times in the NIV New Testament; *treasure* is found twenty-four times.) The Bible does not elaborate upon them. God will reward whatever the believer has achieved for His glory. Similarly, we have no real understanding of the loss that will be experienced in place of rewards not earned. Suffice it to say that God is fair, and His judgment is holy and righteous. Whatever we get, we deserve, and whatever we lose, we deserve to lose.

A careful reading of the New Testament will reveal the degree to which we, as believers, are exhorted to do good deeds, to serve others, to use our gifts and talents wisely, and to invest our lives for eternity.Many specific deeds are named for which rewards are promised, while others can be found for which the believer will be judged and suffer loss at the judgment.

We will be rewarded for doing acts of righteousness (Matt. 6:1), such as giving to the poor (Matt. 10:41); giving someone a cup of cold water (Matt. 10:42); leaving home for the sake of the Gospel (Luke 18:29–30); making disciples (1 Thess.2:19–20); doing good deeds (Gal. 6:9); being generous and willing to share (1 Tim. 6:18–19); and guarding our secret thoughts (Rom. 2:16). Other acts that are wise investments for eternity include showing mercy (James 2:12–13); being kind to children (Matt. 18:5–6); living self-controlled, upright, and godly lives (Titus 2:12); repaying blessing for evil (1 Peter 3:9); and giving ourselves fully to the Lord's work (1 Cor. 15:58).

Some things for which we will suffer loss at the judgment are harming others (2 Tim. 4:14); speaking careless words (Matt. 12:36–37); being ashamed of Christ or His words (Luke 9:26); grumbling against one another (James 5:9); judging or looking down on a fellow believer (Rom. 14:10); and building our lives upon the wrong foundation (1 Cor. 3:10–14).

The conduct of our lives should be constantly influenced by the knowledge that "nothing in all creation is hidden from God's sight.

Everything is uncovered and laid bare before the eyes of him to whom we must give account" (Heb. 4:13).The apostle Paul wrote, "Therefore judge nothing before the appointed time; wait till the Lord comes. He will bring to light what is hidden in darkness and will expose the motives of men's hearts. At that time each will receive his praise from God" (1 Cor. 4:5).

The thought of the judgment seat of Christ is not meant to darken our hope of future blessedness but to stimulate us toward greater faithfulness and obedience. The goal is toward a life marked by complete integrity, so that the outward person—that which is apparent to others—corresponds to the inward. It is only through Christ, through the operation of the Holy Spirit, that this can be realized.

In Hebrews 11, perhaps more than anywhere else in the New Testament, we see the people of God anticipating the rewards and promises of God. Referring to Moses, the writer says, "He regarded disgrace for the sake of Christ as of greater value than the treasures of Egypt, because he was looking ahead to his reward" (Heb. 11:26). Also, "without faith it is impossible to please God, because anyone who comes to him must believe that he exists and that he rewards those who earnestly seek him" (v. 6).

The people listed in this chapter were men and women of faith, still living by faith when they died. "They did not receive the things promised; they only saw them and welcomed them from a distance. And they admitted that they were aliens and strangers on earth" (v. 13). It seems apparent that "the things promised" means more than just spending eternity in heaven.

The doctrine of rewards may be one of the least appreciated by the average Christian. After all, if we are secure in Christ forever, why should we be all that concerned about a judgment that does not even involve punishment? Will it not be enough just to be in heaven? Will not even the least in heaven enjoy the glory of God and the presence of Christ forever? Yet one can hardly ignore a body of teaching that is as pervasive in the scriptures as that of rewards. As stated previously, while we do not fully know the implications of the judgment or the nature of the rewards and loss that believers will experience, we can be sure that they are profound. When Christ returns, we will wish that we had done more in this life for His glory.

CHAPTER 2

SUPPORTING BIBLE PASSAGES

This section contains scripture passages that support the doctrine of rewards, as presented in the previous chapter. It does not include parallel or duplicate passages from the Gospels. There may be other references not listed here, some containing more indirect and perhaps even subtle references to the subject. The verses and passages included in this listing are more than sufficient to demonstrate the degree to which the doctrine of rewards can be found in the Bible.

New Testament

Accountability

Of the parables of Jesus, the following are particularly relevant to the doctrine of rewards. These deal with accountability and stewardship.

Matthew 24:45–51 (Parable: The Faithful and Evil Servants)

> Who then is the faithful and wise servant, whom the master has put in charge of the servants in his household to give them their food at the proper time? It will be good for that servant whose master finds him doing so when he returns. I tell you the truth, he will put him in charge of all his possessions. (vv. 45–47)

While the evil servant in this parable represents a person who has no relationship with Christ, the faithful servant depicts a believer, one who will be awarded privileges and responsibilities consistent with his stewardship.

Matthew 25:14–30 (Parable: The Talents)

> Again, it will be like a man going on a journey, who called his servants and entrusted his property to them. To one he gave five talents of money, to another two talents, and to another one talent, each according to his ability. Then he went on his journey. The man who had received the five talents went at once and put his money to work and gained five more. So also, the one with the two talents gained two more. But the man who had received the one talent went off, dug a hole in the ground and hid his master's money. (vv.14–18)

The servants were given different amounts to steward, based upon each one's ability but with equal responsibility. Those who improved their talents were rewarded accordingly, while those who neglected them were judged for their failure. This is a picture of our individual responsibility to properly steward our God-given gifts, talents, and time, along with eternal accountability to God for that stewardship. No one will be excused for neglecting this duty because he or she has few talents. God will require of us only according to our ability.

Luke 19:12–27 (Parable: The Minas or Pounds)

> He said, "A man of noble birth went to a distant country to have himself appointed king and then to return. So he called ten of his servants and gave them ten minas. 'Put this money to work,' he said, 'until I come back.'" (vv. 12–13)

In this parable, the servants were given equal amounts, with equal responsibility for properly managing them. On the basis of their faithfulness, they would be rewarded with positions of authority in the kingdom.

Romans 14:10–12

> You, then, why do you judge your brother? Or why do you look down on your brother? For we will all stand before God's judgment seat. It is written: "As surely as I live," says the Lord, "every knee will bow before me; every tongue will confess to God." So then, each of us will give an account of himself to God.

2 Corinthians 5:9–10

> So we make it our goal to please him, whether we are at home in the body or away from it. For we must all appear before the judgment seat of Christ, that each one may receive what is due him for the things done while in the body, whether good or bad.

Philippians 4:17

> Not that I am looking for a gift, but I am looking for what may be credited to your account.

Hebrews 13:17

> Obey your leaders and submit to their authority. They keep watch over you as men who must give an account. Obey them so that their work will be a joy, not a burden, for that would be of no advantage to you.

James 3:1

> Not many of you should presume to be teachers, my brothers, because you know that we who teach will be judged more strictly.

1 Peter 4:5

> But they will have to give account to him who is ready to judge the living and the dead.

Sowing and Reaping

The law of the harvest, which applies to all people, Christians and non-Christians alike, says that we will reap what we sow. For Christians, this reaping will occur at the judgment seat of Christ.

Mark 4:24–25

> "Consider carefully what you hear," he continued. "With the measure you use, it will be measured to you-and even more. Whoever has will be given more; whoever does not have, even what he has will be taken from him."

Luke 6:38

> Give, and it will be given to you. A good measure, pressed down, shaken together and running over, will be poured into your lap. For with the measure you use, it will be measured to you.

Luke 8:18

> Therefore consider carefully how you listen. Whoever has will be given more; whoever does not have, even what he thinks he has will be taken from him.

1 Corinthians 3:7–15

> So neither he who plants nor he who waters is anything, but only God, who makes things grow. The man who plants and the man who waters have one purpose, and each will be rewarded according to his own labor. For we are God's fellow workers; you are God's field, God's building. By the grace God has given me, I laid a foundation as an expert builder, and someone else is building on it. But each one should be careful how he builds. For no one can lay any foundation other than the one already laid, which is Jesus Christ. If any man builds on this foundation using gold, silver, costly stones, wood, hay or straw, his work will be shown for what it is, because the Day will bring it to

light. It will be revealed with fire, and the fire will test the quality of each man's work. If what he has built survives, he will receive his reward. If it is burned up, he will suffer loss; he himself will be saved, but only as one escaping through the flames.

2 Corinthians 9:6

Whoever sows sparingly will also reap sparingly, and whoever sows generously will also reap generously.

Galatians 6:7–10

Do not be deceived: God cannot be mocked. A man reaps what he sows. The one who sows to please his sinful nature, from that nature will reap destruction; the one who sows to please the Spirit, from the Spirit will reap eternal life. Let us not become weary in doing good, for at the proper time we will reap a harvest if we do not give up. Therefore, as we have opportunity, let us do good to all people, especially to those who belong to the family of believers.

Ephesians 6:8

You know that the Lord will reward everyone for whatever good he does, whether he is slave or free.

Colossians 3:25

Anyone who does wrong will be repaid for his wrong, and there is no favoritism.

2 Timothy 4:14

Alexander the metalworker did me a great deal of harm. The Lord will repay him for what he has done.

James 3:18

Peacemakers who sow in peace raise a harvest of righteousness.

Revelation 22:12

> Behold, I am coming soon! My reward is with me, and I
> will give to everyone according to what he has done.

Rewards

The following passages refer to specific deeds in this life for which
rewards will be given in heaven.

Matthew 5:3–12

> Blessed are the poor in spirit, for theirs is the kingdom
> of heaven. Blessed are those who mourn, for they will
> be comforted. Blessed are the meek, for they will inherit
> the earth. Blessed are those who hunger and thirst for
> righteousness, for they will be filled. Blessed are the
> merciful, for they will be shown mercy. Blessed are the
> pure in heart, for they will see God. Blessed are the
> peacemakers, for they will be called sons of God. Blessed
> are those who are persecuted because of righteousness,
> for theirs is the kingdom of heaven. Blessed are you when
> people insult you, persecute you and falsely say all kinds
> of evil against you because of me. Rejoice and be glad,
> because great is your reward in heaven, for in the same
> way they persecuted the prophets who were before you.

Matthew 5:46–47

> If you love those who love you, what reward will you get?
> Are not even the tax collectors doing that? And if you
> greet only your brothers, what are you doing more than
> others? Do not even pagans do that?

Matthew 6:1–6

> Be careful not to do your acts of righteousness before men,
> to be seen by them. If you do, you will have no reward
> from your Father in heaven. So when you give to the

needy, do not announce it with trumpets, as the hypocrites do in the synagogues and on the streets, to be honored by men. I tell you the truth, they have received their reward in full. But when you give to the needy, do not let your left hand know what your right hand is doing, so that your giving may be in secret. Then your Father, who sees what is done in secret, will reward you. And when you pray, do not be like the hypocrites, for they love to pray standing in the synagogues and on the street corners to be seen by men. I tell you the truth, they have received their reward in full. But when you pray, go into your room, close the door and pray to your Father, who is unseen. Then your Father, who sees what is done in secret, will reward you.

Matthew 6:16–18

When you fast, do not look somber as the hypocrites do, for they disfigure their faces to show men they are fasting. I tell you the truth, they have received their reward in full. But when you fast, put oil on your head and wash your face, so that it will not be obvious to men that you are fasting, but only to your Father, who is unseen; and your Father, who sees what is done in secret, will reward you.

Matthew 10:41–42

Anyone who receives a prophet because he is a prophet will receive a prophet's reward, and anyone who receives a righteous man because he is a righteous man will receive a righteous man's reward. And if anyone gives even a cup of cold water to one of these little ones because he is my disciple, I tell you the truth, he will certainly not lose his reward.

Matthew 16:27

For the Son of Man is going to come in his Father's glory with his angels, and then he will reward each person according to what he has done.

Mark 9:41

> I tell you the truth, anyone who gives you a cup of water in my name because you belong to Christ will certainly not lose his reward.

Luke 6:35

> But love your enemies, do good to them, and lend to them without expecting to get anything back. Then your reward will be great, and you will be sons of the Most High, because he is kind to the ungrateful and wicked.

Colossians 3:23–24

> Whatever you do, work at it with all your heart, as working for the Lord, not for men, since you know that you will receive an inheritance from the Lord as a reward. It is the Lord Christ you are serving.

Hebrews 10:35–36

> So do not throw away your confidence; it will be richly rewarded. You need to persevere so that when you have done the will of God, you will receive what he has promised.

Hebrews 11:6

> And without faith it is impossible to please God, because anyone who comes to him must believe that he exists and that he rewards those who earnestly seek him.

Hebrews 11:24–27

> By faith Moses, when he had grown up, refused to be known as the son of Pharaoh's daughter. He chose to be mistreated along with the people of God rather than to enjoy the pleasures of sin for a short time. He regarded disgrace for the sake of Christ as of greater value than the treasures of Egypt, because he was looking ahead to

his reward. By faith he left Egypt, not fearing the king's anger; he persevered because he saw him who is invisible.

2 John 8

Watch out that you do not lose what you have worked for, but that you may be rewarded fully.

Treasure

Jesus sometimes spoke of treasures when referring to a believer's rewards in heaven.

Matthew 6:20–21

But store up for yourselves treasures in heaven, where moth and rust do not destroy, and where thieves do not break in and steal. For where your treasure is, there your heart will be also.

Mark 10:21

Jesus looked at him and loved him. "One thing you lack," he said. "Go, sell everything you have and give to the poor, and you will have treasure in heaven. Then come, follow me."

Luke 12:32–34

Do not be afraid, little flock, for your Father has been pleased to give you the kingdom. Sell your possessions and give to the poor. Provide purses for yourselves that will not wear out, a treasure in heaven that will not be exhausted, where no thief comes near and no moth destroys. For where your treasure is, there your heart will be also.

Luke 18:22

> When Jesus heard this, he said to him, "You still lack one thing. Sell everything you have and give to the poor, and you will have treasure in heaven. Then come, follow me."

1Timothy 6:18–19

> Command them to do good, to be rich in good deeds, and to be generous and willing to share. In this way they will lay up treasure for themselves as a firm foundation for the coming age, so that they may take hold of the life that is truly life.

Judgment

In some Bible passages, there may be a blurring of the distinction between who is being judged—the believer or the unbeliever. Yet it is clear that two separate judgments will occur at the coming of Christ: for unbelievers, the Great White Throne judgment described in Revelation 20:11–15; for believers, the judgment seat of Christ.

Matthew 12:36–37

> But I tell you that men will have to give account on the day of judgment for every careless word they have spoken. For by your words you will be acquitted, and by your words you will be condemned.

Matthew 18:5–6

> And whoever welcomes a little child like this in my name welcomes me. But if anyone causes one of these little ones who believe in me to sin, it would be better for him to have a large millstone hung around his neck and to be drowned in the depths of the sea.

Luke 9:23–26

> Then he said to them all: "If anyone would come after me, he must deny himself and take up his cross daily and follow me. For whoever wants to save his life will lose it, but whoever loses his life for me will save it. What good is it for a man to gain the whole world, and yet lose or forfeit his very self? If anyone is ashamed of me and my words, the Son of Man will be ashamed of him when he comes in his glory and in the glory of the Father and of the holy angels."

Romans 2:16

> This will take place on the day when God will judge men's secrets through Jesus Christ, as my gospel declares.

1 Corinthians 11:27–34

> Therefore, whoever eats the bread or drinks the cup of the Lord in an unworthy manner will be guilty of sinning against the body and blood of the Lord. A man ought to examine himself before he eats of the bread and drinks of the cup. For anyone who eats and drinks without recognizing the body of the Lord eats and drinks judgment on himself. That is why many among you are weak and sick, and a number of you have fallen asleep. But if we judged ourselves, we would not come under judgment. When we are judged by the Lord, we are being disciplined so that we will not be condemned with the world. So then, my brothers, when you come together to eat, wait for each other. If anyone is hungry, he should eat at home, so that when you meet together it may not result in judgment.

1 Timothy 5:24–25

> The sins of some men are obvious, reaching the place of judgment ahead of them; the sins of others trail behind them. In the same way, good deeds are obvious, and even those that are not cannot be hidden.

James 2:12–13

> Speak and act as those who are going to be judged by the
> law that gives freedom, because judgment without mercy
> will be shown to anyone who has not been merciful. Mercy
> triumphs over judgment!

James 5:7–9

> Be patient, then, brothers, until the Lord's coming. See
> how the farmer waits for the land to yield its valuable crop
> and how patient he is for the autumn and spring rains. You
> too, be patient and stand firm, because the Lord's coming
> is near. Don't grumble against each other, brothers, or you
> will be judged. The Judge is standing at the door!

1 Peter 4:17

> For it is time for judgment to begin with the family of God;
> and if it begins with us, what will the outcome be for those
> who do not obey the gospel of God?

Rewards Implied

Passages that anticipate the return of Christ often point to the coming
judgment, with the dispensing of rewards and the assignment of loss.

Matthew 7:24–27

> Therefore everyone who hears these words of mine and
> puts them into practice is like a wise man who built his
> house on the rock. The rain came down, the streams rose,
> and the winds blew and beat against that house; yet it did
> not fall, because it had its foundation on the rock. But
> everyone who hears these words of mine and does not put
> them into practice is like a foolish man who built his house
> on sand. The rain came down, the streams rose, and the
> winds blew and beat against that house, and it fell with a
> great crash.

John 6:27

> Do not work for food that spoils, but for food that endures to eternal life, which the Son of Man will give you. On him God the Father has placed his seal of approval.

1 Corinthians 9:7–8

> Who serves as a soldier at his own expense? Who plants a vineyard and does not eat of its grapes? Who tends a flock and does not drink of the milk?

1 Corinthians 15:58

> Therefore, my dear brothers, stand firm. Let nothing move you. Always give yourselves fully to the work of the Lord, because you know that your labor in the Lord is not in vain.

2 Corinthians 4:16–18

> Therefore we do not lose heart. Though outwardly we are wasting away, yet inwardly we are being renewed day by day. For our light and momentary troubles are achieving for us an eternal glory that far outweighs them all. So we fix our eyes not on what is seen, but on what is unseen. For what is seen is temporary, but what is unseen is eternal.

Philippians 2:14–16

> Do everything without complaining or arguing, so that you may become blameless and pure, children of God without fault in a crooked and depraved generation, in which you shine like stars in the universe as you hold out the word of life—in order that I may boast on the day of Christ that I did not run or labor for nothing.

Colossians 3:2–4

> Set your minds on things above, not on earthly things. For you died, and your life is now hidden with Christ in God.

When Christ, who is your life, appears, then you also will appear with him in glory.

Colossians 4:1

Masters, provide your slaves with what is right and fair, because you know that you also have a Master in heaven.

Titus 2:11–14

For the grace of God that brings salvation has appeared to all men. It teaches us to say "No" to ungodliness and worldly passions, and to live self-controlled, upright and godly lives in this present age, while we wait for the blessed hope-the glorious appearing of our great God and Savior, Jesus Christ, who gave himself for us to redeem us from all wickedness and to purify for himself a people that are his very own, eager to do what is good.

Hebrews 12:1

Therefore, since we are surrounded by such a great cloud of witnesses, let us throw off everything that hinders and the sin that so easily entangles, and let us run with perseverance the race marked out for us.

Hebrews 12:10–11

Our fathers disciplined us for a little while as they thought best; but God disciplines us for our good, that we may share in his holiness. No discipline seems pleasant at the time, but painful. Later on, however, it produces a harvest of righteousness and peace for those who have been trained by it.

2 Peter 3:11–13

Since everything will be destroyed in this way, what kind of people ought you to be? You ought to live holy and godly lives as you look forward to the day of God and speed its coming. That day will bring about the destruction of the heavens by fire, and the elements will melt in the heat. But in keeping with his promise we are looking forward to a new heaven and a new earth, the home of righteousness.

Other Expressions

The doctrine of rewards can also be seen in the following passages:

Mark 10:29–31

> "I tell you the truth," Jesus replied, "no one who has left home or brothers or sisters or mother or father or children or fields for me and the gospel will fail to receive a hundred times as much in this present age (homes, brothers, sisters, mothers, children and fields-and with them, persecutions) and in the age to come, eternal life. But many who are first will be last, and the last first."

1 Corinthians 4:5

> Therefore judge nothing before the appointed time; wait till the Lord comes. He will bring to light what is hidden in darkness and will expose the motives of men's hearts. At that time each will receive his praise from God.

1 Corinthians 9:24–27

> Do you not know that in a race all the runners run, but only one gets the prize? Run in such a way as to get the prize. Everyone who competes in the games goes into strict training. They do it to get a crown that will not last; but we do it to get a crown that will last forever. Therefore I do not run like a man running aimlessly; I do not fight like a man beating the air. No, I beat my body and make it my slave so that after I have preached to others, I myself will not be disqualified for the prize.

1 Thessalonians 2:19–20

> For what is our hope, our joy, or the crown in which we will glory in the presence of our Lord Jesus when he comes? Is it not you? Indeed, you are our glory and joy.

1 Timothy 4:8

> For physical training is of some value, but godliness has value for all things, holding promise for both the present life and the life to come.

2 Timothy 4:6–8

> For I am already being poured out like a drink offering, and the time has come for my departure. I have fought the good fight, I have finished the race, I have kept the faith. Now there is in store for me the crown of righteousness, which the Lord, the righteous Judge, will award to me on that day-and not only to me, but also to all who have longed for his appearing.

Titus 3:8

> This is a trustworthy saying. And I want you to stress these things, so that those who have trusted in God may be careful to devote themselves to doing what is good. These things are excellent and profitable for everyone.

Hebrews 6:11–12

> We want each of you to show this same diligence to the very end, in order to make your hope sure. We do not want you to become lazy, but to imitate those who through faith and patience inherit what has been promised.

1 Peter 3:9

> Do not repay evil with evil or insult with insult, but with blessing, because to this you were called so that you may inherit a blessing.

Old Testament

As Christians, we will all stand before the judgment seat of Christ to be rewarded on the basis of how we have lived our lives. Since the Bible is consistent in its teachings, we would expect the Old Testament as well as the New Testament to contain this essential truth. The following are some selected Old Testament passages relating to the doctrine of rewards.

Psalms 19:11

> By them (the ordinances of the Lord) is your servant warned; in keeping them there is great reward.

Proverbs 9:12

> If you are wise, your wisdom will reward you.

Proverbs 11:18

> But he who sows righteousness reaps a sure reward.

Proverbs 13:21

> Misfortune pursues the sinner, but prosperity is the reward of the righteous.

Proverbs 19:17

> He who is kind to the poor lends to the Lord, and he will reward him for what he has done.

Proverbs 25:21–22

> If your enemy is hungry, give him food to eat; if he is thirsty, give him water to drink. In doing this, you will heap burning coals on his head, and the Lord will reward you.

Isaiah 61:8

> For I, the Lord, love justice; I hate robbery and iniquity. In my faithfulness I will reward them and make an everlasting covenant with them.

Jeremiah 17:10

> I the Lord search the heart and examine the mind, to reward a man according to his conduct, according to what his deeds deserve.

Jeremiah 32:19

> Great are your purposes and mighty are your deeds. Your eyes are open to all the ways of men; you reward everyone according to his conduct and as his deeds deserve.

Ecclesiastes 3:17

> God will bring to judgment both the righteous and the wicked, for there will be a time for every activity, a time for every deed.

Ecclesiastes 12:14

> For God will bring every deed into judgment, including every hidden thing, whether it is good or evil.

CHAPTER 3

THE BELIEVER'S CROWNS

The crown was a symbol of victory and reward in the first-century Grecian world. Victors in athletic events received crowns made of leaves, pine needles, ivy, or some other perishable material. Relevant to the doctrine of rewards is the figurative use of crowns in the New Testament. These are special awards promised to believers who persevere in their earthly lives. Just as a crown is worn for all to see, so in heaven, the crowns, in whatever form they may take, will be a testimony to the faithfulness of those who wear them.

Imperishable Crown

"Everyone who competes for the prize is temperate in all things. Now they do it to obtain a perishable crown, but we for an imperishable crown" (1 Cor. 9:25 NKJV). The life we have in Jesus Christ and the rewards we will receive will endure forever.

Crown of Rejoicing

"For what is our hope, or joy, or crown of rejoicing? Is it not even you in the presence of our Lord Jesus Christ at His coming" (1 Thess. 2:19 NKJV). Perhaps nothing will cause us to rejoice more when Christ returns than the presence of others in heaven who are there as a result of our labor, who themselves are receiving rewards at the judgment seat of Christ.

Crown of Life

"Blessed is the man who perseveres under trial, because when he has stood the test, he will receive the crown of life that God has promised to those who love him" (James 1:12). Even though neither our love nor our faith gains us eternal life, the Bible teaches that God will abundantly bless those who love Him, keep His commandments, and serve Him faithfully, whatever the cost may be. The crown of life is nothing less than eternal life itself and all that accompanies it.

Crown of Righteousness

"Now there is in store for me the crown of righteousness, which the Lord, the righteous Judge, will award to me on that day-and not only to me, but also to all who have longed for his appearing" (2 Tim. 4:8). Like the crown of life, the crown of righteousness is righteousness itself, imputed to all who love Christ and await His return.

Crown of Glory

"And when the Chief Shepherd appears, you will receive the crown of glory that will never fade away" (1 Peter 5:4). The glory that is Christ's will be ours, with a special measure given perhaps to those who shepherd God's people in a worthy manner.

Printed in the United States
by Baker & Taylor Publisher Services